A World of Good

A World of Good. First Edition.

Cover design by Ricky Hill

Book design by Gethin Nadin

Proof Reading by Sophie Gane

Profile Photography by Tina Downham

Published independently by Gethin Nadin. First Printing November 2017.

Credits and permissions are listed on page 229 and are considered a continuation of the copyright page.

ISBN: 9781973937937

18 19 20 21 22 10 9 8 7 6 5 4 3 2

A World of Good

Lessons From Around the World in Improving the Employee Experience

Gethin Nadin

Within a few months of its release in November 2017, 'A World of Good' was listed on Amazon UK's Top Ten bestselling HR books with a 5-star rating. I'm forever humbled and grateful for all the support this book has had.

"Gethin has been in the vanguard of Employee Engagement for as long as I can remember. As someone whose finger is firmly on the pulse of workplace innovation, this book is an incredible culmination of his learnings from the past decade."

- *Ry Morgan, Co-Founder and CPO at Unmind*

"An empowering read, in a time when much of what we read is doom and gloom this great book holds up a brilliant light in the darkness."

- *Ruth Steggles, Founder, Fresh Air Fridays*

"If you truly want to create greatness for your people, buy this book."

- *Kelly Swingler, Founder & Rulebreaker at Chrysalis Consulting*

"A great read and a great message to the world."

- *Ben Whitter, Founder, World Employee Experience Institute*

ABOUT THE AUTHOR

Gethin Nadin is a psychology graduate who has worked in Employee Benefits, Employee Engagement and Employee Experience for more than 15 years. Gethin has helped some of the world's largest and most recognisable brands to improve their workplaces for the better. A frequent commentator, speaker and lecturer, Gethin has been featured in The Financial Times, The Guardian and The Huffington Post. Gethin has also been a judge at numerous Employee Experience, HR and Customer Experience awards.

DEDICATIONS

This book is dedicated to my Mother and Father. They taught me to bring as much good into the world as I can, and so I wish them all the good in the world. This book is also dedicated to my partner Luke for his love, support and encouragement in everything I do.

I would also like to thank my amazing group of close friends who are always there to encourage me. Writing this book has been as challenging as it has been enlightening.

PREFACE

As politics pulls us further apart from other cultures, I think it's important for us to remember that, collectively, we have the power to bring about real change in the world. In 1894, New Zealand established the first minimum wage; in 1964 America introduced the Civil Rights Act that ensured all employees were treated equally, and in 1974, Sweden introduced cross-gender parental leave. These localised workplace changes paved the way for the rest of the world to follow.

"Cultural differences should not separate us from each other, but rather cultural diversity brings a collective strength that can benefit all of humanity"

- Robert Alan

I wrote this book because I truly believe we can make the world and the workplace better. Finding ways to improve the lives of employees should be a priority for every employer. Employees are human, and they aren't resources. As we see the end of the traditional HR department, more than ever, an organisation's front line affects their bottom line.

G. Nadin

Gethin Nadin, November 5th, 2017, London

ACKNOWLEDGMENTS

I would like to thank all the amazing researchers, psychologists and organisations that have dedicated so much time and effort to improving the workplace. Also, thank you to those HR and wellbeing experts from all over the world, who took the time to be interviewed for this book. Your insights have been invaluable.

Scott Baker, Reward Consultant & Co-Founder at Road to Green Ltd

Jackie Buttery, Former Global Head of Reward and Benefits at Herbert Smith Freehills, now independent consultant

Nick Court, Founder and CEO of Cloud9 People

Joanne Crovini, Nutritional Therapist & Workplace Wellbeing Specialist

Samantha Gee, Former HR Director & Reward Consultant, Founder of Verditer Consulting

Nick Gianoulis, Founder & 'Godfather of Fun' at The Fun Dept. and co-author of Playing It Forward

Gemma Godfrey, TV money expert & Founder & CEO of Moola

Peter Jenkinson, Business Development Director, Wrkit

Kathryn Kendall, Chief People Officer, Benefex

Mike Minett, Founder & Managing Director of The Positive Ageing Company (a Mercer brand)

ACKNOWLEDGMENTS

Ry Morgan, Co-Founder & CPO, Unmind

Chris Orrell, CEO & Founder of the Travel Circus Ltd & HotelVoucherShop.com

Patrick Phelan, Co-Founder at The Happiness Index

Ruth Steggles, Founder of Fresh Air Fridays

Jo Thresher, Director of Better with Money

Ben Whitter, 'Mr Employee Experience' & Founder, World Employee Experience Institute (WEEI)

I'd also like to thank the following organisations for their support in publicising this book; **Benefex**, **Chrysalis Consulting**, **Incentive & Motivation Magazine**, **Kina'ole Canada**, **The Employee Engagement Alliance**, **People Management Magazine**, **ProShare**, **Randstad**, **Sage People**, **The People Experience Hub and 4PS Marketing**.

Finally, I'd like to thank Matt Macri-Waller for enouraging me to thrive in the world of HR technology. By being an inspiring and supportive leader, a friend and the best manager I've ever had, Matt has helped me have my own amazing employee experience. Working for Matt and all of the great organisations and colleagues I have over the last 15 years, has really given my career purpose.

A World of Good

CONTENTS

1. Introduction

The employee is in control

From an early age, the expectation to work and earn our place in society is ingrained in us. Our wellbeing relies on working to contribute to society as the negative effects of unemployment range from poor mental health[1] to higher mortality rates[2]. Whether we're working in a city office or driving around the countryside, for most of us, working will be the only way we can ensure there is a roof over our head and food in our bellies. Work has become the primary reason most of us wake up in the morning.

If you ever find yourself on a game show, one of the first questions a host will ask is, "what do you do?". Society has determined that our work should play a big part in defining who we are and an even bigger part of our daily lives. It is suggested that we will spend around a third of our lives just working[3]. However, for lots of us, work has started to represent something more than just a way of earning money.

Work offers us unique opportunities for social engagement, a sense of achievement, and the ability to learn. For many, it has become a way of giving real meaning to their lives. One of the greatest decisions we make in our lives will be what we decide to do for a job, and what we hope to achieve by doing it.

We can all remember answering that nursery school question, “what do you want to be when you grow up?”. Since we can’t all be astronauts and firefighters, we need to refine our decisions once we’ve experienced work for the first time.

As work became more than just earning money, Governments around the world started to regulate the workplace. However, most of the laws that govern our workplaces today have been around for a long, long time. From the Trade Disputes Act 1906 to the Old Age Pensions Act 1908, the turn of the last century was a boom time for workplace changes. But a lot can change in 100 years. In 1915, life expectancy was just 47 years and only eight per cent of the US had a telephone[4]. By the end of the second World War, more than 80 per cent of the UK workforce belonged (in some way) to a union and the fight for the fair treatment of employees was underway. The things the Government tried to protect us from 100 years ago aren’t the same things we need protecting from today.

Since the middle of the last century, the growing trend to improve the workplace led psychologists to study the effect it has on people. Thousands of studies have been dedicated to improving the world of work for both employees and employers. In recent years, this trend has grown rapidly as the modern employer reacts to a change in expectation from society.

Throughout this book, we'll consider almost 400 facts, research articles and exclusive interviews to find out why the workplace is changing so much, and what employers can do to keep up with it. The world of work is changing, and the lessons we can learn from other - sometimes more progressive - countries is invaluable. In a speech a few years ago, Sir Christopher Bland, chairman of BT Group, warned; "Western companies will be at the mercy of tiger economies, such as China and India, unless they adopt better working practices"[5].

How employees are treated varies hugely around the world. Some countries protect their employees' weekends by law (like Greece and Estonia), whereas others have very high minimum wages (like Turkey). Quartz Media looked at how long employees would have to work to be able to buy a Big Mac[6]. The variation is astonishing. Mexicans would have to work for almost 45 minutes to be able to buy a Big Mac, whereas Australians only have to work 8 minutes. Australian employees could buy six more Big Macs an hour than their Mexican counterparts. It is this variation in working conditions that gives us the ideas proposed in this book. There are lessons to be learnt everywhere. Not even the most progressive countries get everything right. For example, for all their progressive ideas (some detailed in this book), Americans have zero paid leave – the only country in the world not to have any state fixed paid leave.

As the world becomes a smaller place, the workplace is increasingly dominated by younger workers. A new wave of global employers, like Facebook and Google, bring with them a different attitude to the employee/employer relationship. Gone are the days when an employee was happy just to be paid, as more workers focus on the other benefits of employment.

HR thought leader Simon Sinek says, "taking a job for the cash is not as important as taking a job for the joy", and this represents the feelings of many employees in 2017. The move away from being a money-orientated employee is a good one, as research shows that many of us are unhappy with what we are paid. Adzuna found that two out of five employees believe they are paid less than their colleagues, with the unhappiest workers being in retail[7]. The tides have changed, and the employee now has the power to decide if a job is right for them. The employee is now the consumer, and the job is the product. It's now the employer's turn to convince employees to come and work for them.

Employers need to add value to the task of working every day and make the workplace a more enticing place to be. Those employers who no longer look out for the welfare of their employees can expect to see their working practices made public and scrutinised by all on social media and employer review sites. In the 21st century, employment has now become so transparent that public opinion of certain organisations has started to seriously affect their bottom line.

In their 2017 report, Talent 2021, consulting form AON say that the youngest employees see their careers from a very different angle to their employer[8]. "There are no pensions, not a lot of career growth, and miniscule pay increases. The average Millennial may work for an employer for a couple of years and then want to move on". These young, enthusiastic employees are motivated by progression rather than pay check and so an organisation's culture is more important than ever to get right. In a phrase first coined by Peter Drucker and later made famous by the president of Ford, "culture eats strategy for breakfast, lunch and dinner" has become synonymous with successful organisations.

Even for those who are motivated by money, or realise that there is a certain standard of living they need to be funding, the workplace just isn't the same place it was. In the 21st century, it has never been easier for an employee to find a new job, which means it has never been harder for an employer to keep hold of them. For many employees, staying in the same job just doesn't offer the same development and financial benefits it used to, so they're keen to move on. In fact, according to Forbes, staying employed at the same company for more than two years is likely to see an employee earn around 50 per cent less in their working life than if they moved jobs[9]. The average wage rise an employee can expect this year is around three per cent. The rise they can expect by switching job sits at an average of 15 per cent[10].

Over the last 15 years, we've seen huge generational changes in the workplace. The Baby Boomers knuckled down to bring the UK back to its feet after World War Two, and the country finally welcomed women to become part of the working majority. As Britain moved away from the post-war era, more younger employees benefitted from a boom in industry, a stable economy and a relatively comfortable existence. However, a new wave of economic downturns and terror attacks have rocked the stability of younger generations, and brought about a more socially conscious, digital-native employee with much higher expectations of work than ever before. These younger employees have arrived in the workplace with a very different background to those who went before them. A once quiet and comfortable generation was rocked by large-scale terror attacks and a banking crisis that brought fear and uncertainty to their lives. With these changes came the knowledge that a job for life no longer exists, but a new desire to make a real difference to their world.

An employee in 2017 is an employee who is more open-minded and relaxed than any we've seen in a long time, and this is great for employers. Samantha Gee, former HR Director and Reward Specialist, and Founder of Verditer Consulting told me, "although the concept of a 'job for life' has gone and the frequency of employees moving between employers is growing, an employer who can operate as a 'company for life' will benefit".

The needs and wants of younger employees must to be taken seriously. By 2020, Millennials (those born after 1980) will be the largest generation in the workplace and account for more than half of all employees. Despite their parents benefitting from 'jobs for life' and long-term security, these new employees come to work with a very different agenda. PwC's Reshaping the Workplace report reveals that over a quarter of younger employees expect to have six or more employers in their lifetime[11]. That figure was just 10 per cent, 10 years ago. Rising costs and student loans have left younger employees with huge debt and little confidence in their financial future. This has led many to compromise over the job they take, just to make ends meet. PwC reports that these tough times have forced many to make tradeoffs to get into work. Graduates report taking 'any job' just to start paying their bills and getting stuck in a job they didn't intend to take, or is unrelated to their specialist education. These compromises mean it's becoming much harder to retain good employees, and voluntary turnover is certain to increase as worldwide economic conditions improve. Almost half of all younger workers say they are actively looking for a different role[12].

In 2017, more than one in four employees blamed work as the primary cause of their poor mental health. It's estimated this is losing 12 billion working days every year and is costing the world's economy more than £650 billion[13]. It's now at epidemic levels and the employer is having to step up. Employers now realise that to get employees at their best, they must support them when they're at their worst.

The culture of a nine-to-five and a dictatorial boss won't cut it anymore and employees won't put up with it. The ability to move away from a toxic boss or workplace so easily is putting pressure on employers to create a compassionate and supportive working environment.

I spoke to Ben Whitter, 'Mr Employee Experience' himself, and founder, World Employee Experience Institute (WEEI), about the future of work. Whitter told me, "companies are finding out the hard way that the true costs associated with a poor workplace are unbearable. Yes, research is showing that investing in the employee experience has a positive impact on profitability, productivity and customer satisfaction, but we also see examples every single day that demonstrate the clear consequences of not providing good experiences for staff within work". Whitter says these poor employee experiences are putting companies out of business, smashing stock prices, and affecting consumer confidence. Whitter adds, "we have, as consumers, been given more choice, more ability to call out poor practices or bad examples of customer service. Now, it is the turn of employers to lead the charge in the creation of a more human-centred and meaningful economy".

Having worked in Employee Benefits, Engagement and Experience organisations for more than 15 years, I've worked with a lot of employees and employers from all over the world. My experience tells me that nobody wakes up and goes to work to do anything other than the best they can.

I believe the modern employee understands that they will devote a sizable portion of their lives to working, and so has made the decision to get as much out of working as possible. Time is something we have a finite amount of, and something that once spent, we can never get back. By giving their employer their time, employees are giving them something valuable, and money alone can't compensate for that. The American jazz musician Lionel Hampton described most people's attitude to work when he said, "the secret is keeping busy and loving what you do".

As a nation, our work - combined with a drive to be productive - can have huge economic effects. In the UK, our productivity lags behind that of other major economies. The Office for Budget Responsibility (OBR) warned us that UK productivity growth would be lower than expected and return to just two per cent by 2020. If the UK's productivity growth had maintained its course from 1997 onwards, it would be sitting at around 17 per cent more than it currently does. Economic downturns, the rise of zero-hour contracts, and political instability have all contributed to our slow productivity growth.

Employers and employees alike need to look at ways of increasing productivity to deliver economic benefit to the whole of the UK. Attracting and retaining staff as well as keeping them as engaged as possible has never been so important. Staff are now widely considered to be an investment, not a cost, as major organisations around the world realise how vital good employees are to their overall success.

Some of the most forward-thinking organisations in the world realise how much value employees can add. Google encourages all employees to spend 20 per cent of their time working on what they think will best benefit Google. Tapping into this kind of 'Intrepreneurship' (entrepreneurs working inside an organisation) has really paid off. Google's flagship email product, Gmail, came from one employee using their 20 per cent time. Other products that were designed by employees who were encouraged to be innovative included Post-It notes and the Sony Playstation. Like Google, the Microsoft Garage is an internal project division at Microsoft that lets employees work on any projects they like. Just like at Google, it has produced some impressive products like Snip. Forward thinking employers are already realising that every employee is a much more than just what their job title says.

Recruiting, retaining and engaging the best workers is now the only way an employer can ensure organisational success. There is simply no other way to build a successful, sustainable business anymore. Countless studies reveal that just a small proportion of a workforce will drive a substantial proportion of an organisations results[14]. The top one per cent of a company's best performing employees will account for 10 per cent of your entire organisational output. The top 20 per cent will account for a massive 80 per cent. If employers don't care for and invest in their people, they'll soon realise the negative effects. The future of work is all about employee wellbeing, and it is coming whether employers are ready for it or not.

Recently, executive boards started to realise the importance of caring for their employees. In 2015, founder of the Virgin Group Sir Richard Branson, famously declared; "Take care of your employees and they'll take care of your business". Since then, employee engagement became a big focus for Human Resources. With what was probably one of the most widely adopted trends in recent years, every significant organisation around the world attempted to improve their employee engagement. Branson has positioned himself and the Virgin brand at the forefront of employee engagement and wellbeing for several years. Branson once said, "your employees are your company's real competitive advantage. They're the ones making the magic happen – so long as their needs are being met". As more and more employers realised the importance of employee engagement, some thought leaders were starting to focus on something different, something more intrinsic to the employee; the employee experience.

Deloitte's 2017 Global Human Capital Trends report reveals that 79 per cent of global employers believe the employee experience is important or very important to the future of work[15]. More important than diversity and inclusion, people analytics, digital HR and performance management. It's one of the most significant and important trends we've seen in the workplace for many years.

The employee experience is of particular importance to emerging and developed economies including Latin and South America, North America, Africa and Europe.

Some of the world's leading organisations have focused on the employee experience over the past few years with momentous success. In his book The Employee Experience Advantage, author Jacob Morgan explains what his research reveals to make for the best employee experience.

Morgan identifies three principal areas:

- **Cultural:** The feeling employees get at work
- **Physical:** The actual space in which they work
- **Technological:** The tools employees use at work

The Employee Experience Index by IBM found a direct link between the performance and retention of employees and their overall employee experience[16]. IBM found that employees who feel a sense of belonging in an organisation and are happy, contribute, "above and beyond" expectations.

This book will focus on helping employers improve their workplace and culture through lessons from different countries around the world. Human Resources has never had more attention from executive boards and employees have never needed HR as much as they do today.

When I interviewed Ben Whitter, 'Mr Employee Experience', founder, World Employee Experience Institute (WEEI), he explained how employers and employees are working together like never before. "This employee-led transformation is challenging employers of all sizes to intentionally define, design, and deliver compelling experiences in work. Certainly, in our work at the World Employee Experience Institute, we are seeing organisations across the world investing in and co-creating the employee experience with their staff. Imagine that. Employer and employees working in harmony to create something truly remarkable for each other, their customers and their communities". Whitter adds, "this might seem like common sense, but it is an approach that has not been commonly applied across the economy… yet. With a focus on the employee experience, we have the key to unlock the potential and energy within our workplaces, everywhere". The significant impact that HR can now have on the lives of their employees should not be underestimated.

In the film The Great Dictator, Charlie Chaplin's character Adenoid Hynkel gives a rousing speech which includes the line, "you, the people have the power… The power to create happiness! You, the people, have the power to make this life free and beautiful, to make this life a wonderful adventure". It's a speech that has always stuck with me. I believe that part of the employee experience is to understand your employees as people and to build an emotional connection with them.

I wrote this book because people have the power to affect real change in the world and as HR professionals, managers and colleagues, we can do that at work. We should all be doing whatever we can to help improve the lives of our fellow employees. It's not just the job of HR.

This book aims to share ideas and thoughts on making the workplace a happier place to be, and to help employers create their very own world of good.

2. Fika

Sweden

In Sweden (and Finland) there is a specific name for 'having coffee' (usually accompanied by pastries) called 'Fika'. The word can be used as a verb or a noun, so Swedes frequently 'fika at work'. Its origins can be traced back to the 19th century and the word derives from the Swedish for coffee, 'kaffe'. In Sweden, its popularity has increased in 2017 with the release of the viral video 'Swedish Fika' by Oskar Kongshöj and Gustaf Mardelius.

Fika has become a bit of a social institution in Scandinavia, and is very popular in the workplace in particular; employees will generally fika at least once a day. However, unlike the traditional coffee break we see in the UK and the US, senior management will often join employees to discuss anything – whether it's work related or not. This is where the practice can teach us a lot about improving the employee experience.

For a long time, many psychologists theorised that if we got distracted from a task at work, that would impede our ability to focus on it again. However, a lot of modern research contradicts this. The Journal of Cognition examined what they called 'vigilance décrément' (a reduction in our ability to pay attention)[17].

Human attention span was previously thought of as a resource that was limited and could be used up. However, the authors of this research now suggest that it's the result of stopping paying attention, not losing attention that's the problem. Our attention spans are finite, so they require us to take breaks to recharge.

To test this theory, University of Illinois psychology professor Alejandro Lleras and his colleague Atsunori Ariga tested people's ability to focus when completing a repetitive computer task for one hour[18]. The study split 84 participants into four different groups. The first was the control group who performed the task without any breaks or diversions. The second and third were the switch group, and non-switch group. Each of these groups memorised four digits prior to performing the task. They were then asked to respond if they saw one of the digits on screen during the test. All groups were then tested on their ability to recall these digits at the end of the task. The last group was called the digit-ignored group. This group was shown the same four digits but told to ignore them.

As expected, most of the participants' performances declined throughout the task. However, those in the switch group saw no drop in their performance at all. Having the participants take two brief breaks from their task (to respond to the digits on screen) allowed them to stay focused during the entire experiment. These types of frequent breaks that make us switch tasks and concentration have also shown to improve creativity[19].

As well as taking a formal break from work, research has also looked at the benefits of allowing our minds to wander.

We spend almost 50 per cent of our time thinking about something that isn't the thing we are doing[20]. This kind of mind wandering can be damaging, so using mindfulness to focus our attention can be a fantastic way to relax our minds. Over the last 10 years, a lot of attention has been paid to mindfulness, and the benefits of taking stock of your thoughts. Ruth Steggles, founder of Fresh Air Fridays explains how mindfulness works; "The entry-level take that we have on mindfulness is that most people spend most of their time ruminating about things in the past that could have gone differently or worrying about or looking forward to what may or may not happen in the future. The only thing that any of us has is this very moment. When we break this moment down into the smallest fraction of time, we find that we are alright".

It's suggested that not addressing mindfulness at work could cost British businesses more than £101 billion by 2030[21]. Ry Morgan, Co-Founder and CPO at Unmind, thinks mindfulness is also about prevention. "For me, it's imperative that businesses move away from a solely reactionary model of mental health support and begin to offer proactive solutions too. Doing so provides a net commercial benefit to the organisation and, more importantly, an enormous emotional impact to staff – including friends or family around them". Morgan thinks employees should be using technology to practice mindfulness when taking a break from work.

Morgan says, "excitingly, modern technology enables businesses of any size to rollout solutions of this nature to their workforce – empowering staff to look after their wellbeing anytime, anywhere, on any device".

Professor Kalina Christoff at the Department of Psychology at the University of British Columbia states in her research, "mind wandering is typically associated with negative things like laziness or inattentiveness". Christoff published a study in the Proceedings of the National Academy of Sciences[22] and found that various parts of the brain increase in activity when we let our minds wander. For Christoff's study, participants were placed inside an fMRI scanner while they completed the simple task of pushing a button when numbers appeared on a screen. The researchers measured participants' attentiveness through brain scans, reports from the participants themselves, and by tracking the results of the task.

As Christoff's findings outline, "daydreaming is an important cognitive state where we may unconsciously turn our attention from immediate tasks to sort through important problems in our lives". Interestingly, the study also found that the brain's 'executive network' (usually associated with complex problem-solving) also becomes active when we daydream. The extent of this brain activity suggests that employees struggling to concentrate and solve problems at work should consider 'switching off' or focusing on simpler tasks for short periods, thus achieving better results.

In 1955 Jerome L. Singer published a (now frequently referenced) study into the effects of daydreaming. A common theme of his research was something called 'Positive Constructive Daydreaming' (PCD). PCD refers to a specific type of daydreaming where people focus on playful, wishful, and constructive imagery. Research by Singer has given a wealth of evidence that points to daydreaming as being proof of a healthy mind. Being able to let our minds rest gives us the opportunity to self-reflect, which can lead to improved creativity. Steggles adds, "in a practical sense, mindfulness helps us to become calmer, less overwhelmed, more aware and better able to respond than react. By encouraging this kind of awareness, employers can invite employees to try something that at least could be relaxing and calming, but could also be potentially profound for anyone willing to take time to explore it".

It makes sense to take focus away from work and allow our mind to 'rest' before using it again. Although the brain isn't technically a muscle, it does behave like one. There are several ways to give our brains a work-out and subsequently recover, but an easy one is for us to simply socialise more. Although taking a break from a screen or a task is effortless, socialising at work has never been more of a challenge. As more and more employers encourage remote and home working, and as more of our tasks are completed using technology, the human touch of the workplace has become a much trickier thing to achieve.

Jackie Buttery, Former Global Head of Reward and Benefits at Herbert Smith Freehills, now an independent consultant, thinks we should be encouraging our employees to interact outside of traditional work meetings. "Formal meetings can be so short and so sterile at times. To have greater time with people we have a work connection with can give us the opportunity to stop and think, to hear what's important in the other person's world and to mix in an informal setting. Such time is precious. The learnings we can take from such interactions can be massive". Psychologist Susan Pinker agrees and believes that our inability to build relationships at work is having a negative impact on employee mental health.

In the book The Village Effect, Pinker shows that human contact at work is important, and creating our own personal 'village' makes us happier. When we connect physically with other people (like a simple handshake), oxytocin is released in the brain. This chemical promotes feelings of attachment and trust. In the workplace, this can have obvious positive implications on collaboration and team building. Increased social contact at work has also shown to reduce the production of cortisol - the chemical we release when we're stressed. Fika gives employees a unique opportunity to spend time with colleagues, away from work related chat.

A 2012 study published in BMC Public Health[23] showed that when employees feel like they're bonding, their stress levels decrease. Decreased stress means employees are less likely to burn out, and more likely to be productive.

Spending time with our colleagues socially gives us the opportunity to bond and have fun. Since David Brent first arrived on UK television screens, the idea of having a funny boss has been met with cringes from employees. However, fun at work is an important part of our overall engagement. Managers can use humour as a stress management tool and can even improve the cohesiveness of a team using it[24].

In the study It Pays to Play, Professor Sir Gary Cooper surveyed 2,000 UK employees and found that those progressive organisations who encourage fun, socialising and laughter had employees who were more productive, happier and satisfied at work[25]. The Walt Disney Company believes that laughter has such a positive impact, they have a programme dedicated to filling hospital rooms with laughter[26]. Encouraging employees to fika regularly isn't just about benefitting their own mental health and wellbeing; it makes business sense.

If an employee's ability to focus is impeded by their own cognitive incapacity, employers should be encouraging regular breaks to improve productivity. Although the Swedes and the Finnish only take a few fikas a day, there is growing research into how many we should be taking for optimum impact. Social scientists suggest that to achieve maximum productivity at work, we should be taking one 17-minute break to every 52 minutes we work[27]. This number of suggested breaks is far more than what is outlined by the UK Working Time Regulations of 1998, which enforce only one 21-minute break for more than six hours worked.

It seems unfair by today's standards, but it is still the law, despite being made almost 20 years ago. Twenty years is a long time. Twenty years ago, we didn't have smartphones, social media, e-books or YouTube. All of these things have significantly changed our lives and moulded a generation. The world of work has come a long way in two decades, and our practices need to be redesigned accordingly. Considering how long it takes for new laws to come into force, the immediate responsibility is falling on employers to make the changes voluntarily. Aside from the productivity and social aspects, taking a break from work can also increase an employee's creative ability.

Researchers from the Columbia Business School[28] looked at the impact of switching tasks. Although lots of research in this area points towards the negative effects of swapping between tasks; in several experiments, the researchers uncovered an upside – in reducing cognitive fixation, our ability to be creative can enhance. In this study, participants who continually alternated between two creativity-based tasks outperformed those who switched at their discretion or at set intervals. Their findings suggest that people can improve their creativity when navigating multiple creative tasks.

If breaking from work every hour to chat with colleagues isn't going to work in your organisation, employees could just open a new browser and start looking at pictures of kittens instead. This unusual approach comes from Japan, where researchers showed pictures of fluffy baby animals to employees to see how it boosted productivity.

Researchers from Hiroshima University[29] showed students pictures of baby animals before they completed various tasks. The research found that the students who had seen the pictures were more productive afterwards than those who hadn't. The theory is that the pictures ignite our inherent nurturance. Caring for small animals (or babies) requires careful attention, and so the performance of the students' non-motor perceptual tasks was improved.

Allowing employees to take a break from work more regularly is about ensuring they are fit to work and not overwhelmed. Our minds need rest to be able to operate effectively. A tired or unfocused employee will never deliver the best customer service, or the highest quality work they can. Encouraging employees to take regular breaks to socialise will ensure they are refreshed, relaxed, and more connected with their colleagues.

3. Ikigai

Japan

Something that has always frustrated me about people's attitude to work is that we are constantly told 'do what you love'. For many that might be singing, acting or art. Not many of us grow up dreaming of working on a checkout, in an office or collecting rubbish. Asking people to follow what they love as a career choice assumes that their desires lie in one thing, are static and are almost intrinsic. For most of us, we will end up doing a job we didn't plan for, or necessarily wanted when we dreamt about growing up - and that's ok. People need to start realising that their passion can change throughout their life and exists within themselves, not in a job. Most of us need to work to stay alive and we aren't all lucky enough to do a job we love. However, I do believe we can grow to like (at least) parts of our job, so we can 'love what we do' instead. In Japanese, giving ourselves a good reason to get up in the morning and go to work is called 'Ikigai'.

Ikigai is roughly translated from Japanese as 'a reason for being'. Finding our Ikigai isn't always an easy thing to do and requires a lot of self-discovery. However, the Japanese believe by doing so we can bring satisfaction to our lives.

The term Ikigai is made up of two Japanese words; iki (meaning life, and Kai, which means, "the realisation of what one expects and hopes for". You can find out what your own Ikigai might be by looking at the diagram below:

Finding ways to make work more enjoyable or successful requires us to look back at what we've achieved so far. Thinking about what we have achieved to date and how they made us feel is a great first step in realising what skills we have, and more importantly the skills we enjoy having, rather than looking at the end goal.

Some of the best sales people I've ever met didn't grow up wanting to work in sales (does anyone?), but the opportunity gives them the chance to use their skills in negotiating, networking and relationship-building. Many of them now enjoy their jobs immensely and have benefitted financially from a change in career direction.

The University of Michigan thinks that achieving passion for our work is something we can develop over time[30]. The idea that we can only achieve passion for the right kind of work (what the researchers call 'fit theory') is fast being debunked as psychologists suggest we really can learn to love our jobs (also known as 'develop theory'). We are frequently reminded that if we are going to do it for eight hours a day, we should try to do a job we enjoy. However, psychology researcher Patricia Chen thinks that isn't the only way. "The good news is that we can choose to change our beliefs or strategies to cultivate passion gradually or seek compatibility from the outset, and be just as effective in the long run at achieving this coveted experience", said Chen.

Chen conducted four separate studies where she surveyed participants on their attitude to work and looked at their career expectations with regards to both fit theory and develop theory[31]. Chen discovered that regardless of which theory the participants' career choices embodied, their level of passion ended up being the same. Chen says, "people can achieve similar levels of well-being at work by endorsing either the fit or develop theory".

The significant difference between the two is in how outcomes are reached. Chen believes that fit theorists choose specific lines of work that fit them early on in their careers, whereas develop theorists grow into that fit over time.

In the 1980s, Steve Jobs tried to lure John Sculley to leave Pepsi Co. and to become the new CEO of Apple. Apparently, Jobs asked Sculley, "do you want to spend the rest of your life selling sugared water or do you want a chance to change the world?". Sculley took the job because doing so meant he was part of something. Recently, one of the world's largest employers, Facebook, considered what made their employees excited to come to work, and what gives their work meaning. An internal study conducted by the Facebook HR team and Wharton Professor Adam Grant[32], revealed that pride in the company is what makes their employees more satisfied, committed and successful.

Facebook recognises that pride takes a crucial role in our lives inside and outside of work. From graduation to having a child, many of the landmark points in our lives give us satisfaction because they are things we can be proud of. There's even a physiological response to being proud as it spikes our testosterone[33]. In their study, Facebook theorised that pride in a company or a role is achieved through three main factors:

- **Optimism** – How much do employees believe in the future of the company?
- **Mission** – How much do employees care about the company?
- **Social good** – Is the company making the world a better place?

Facebook found that these factors drove pride regardless of the job their employees did, or which department they worked in. Employers should really think about how they can aid social good. Pride in their company is the reason Facebook's employees wake up and go to work.

As we've already seen, the modern workforce dominated by younger employees demands so much more than just money. They are more emotive and socially conscious than any generation that has gone before them. Employees want to work for an organisation that is going to make them feel good about themselves, and working for a socially good organisation can really help to achieve that. Ultimately, this will satisfy part of their Ikigai. This has become so strong that younger workers are shying away from certain industries like finance and defence as their social conscience plays a big part in their career choices[34].

Older workers are also seeing a shift in what they look for in their work.

As retirement ages get pushed back and state-sponsored benefits for the elderly become less available, we have seen a huge increase in the number of older employees in the workplace.

As of April 2017, the employment rate for people aged 50 to 69 in the UK was 59 per cent. HR Magazine reports that by 2020 the over-50s will compromise almost a third of the working population[35]. In the US, American workers aged 55 years and over are expected to grow to nearly 20 per cent of the entire workforce by 2025[36]. People's longer lives and longer working lives mean that, although the workforce might be dominated by younger workers, there is a still a high proportion of older workers who need to be considered. What is surprising is that these older employees are also shifting what they look for in their work. Older employees also want to be more socially conscious.

In early 2017, the Centre for Ageing Better released a new study, which focused on understanding what older employees want and value in their work, to help them work for longer[37]. The researchers found that what older generations value in the workplace doesn't differ very much from that of younger workers: meaningful work. The report found that older workers are more likely to feel engaged at work when they believe their work is worthwhile.

It seems that finding our Ikigai is just as important in later life as it is when we are younger.

Evidentially, older employees find work fulfilling when they're able to help others. Most older workers are likely to seek out work that enables them to pass on their vast knowledge and experience onto younger employees. As we'll find out later this book, the knowledge sharing of older workers can have huge benefits to the whole workforce.

For years, studies on people's happiness and satisfaction have pointed towards altruism as a sure-fire way to lead a more contented life. In a survey of the top tech companies from around the world, employees reported finding their daily work most meaningful at Facebook, Tesla, Google, Apple and SpaceX[38]. Social good forms a fundamental part of the company mission for each of these companies. Interestingly, a recent study suggests that giving social support to other people benefits the giver more than the receiver.

Researchers from the University of Pittsburgh and University of California used fMRI brain scanning to pinpoint specific brain benefits of helping others[39]. Participants in the study were asked to recall scenarios in which they gave or received help from others. The fMRI scans showed specific activation of these areas of the brain when giving, but not receiving support from others. The findings of this and other similar studies confirm that there are overall health benefits to giving support to others, and highlights that these are probably biological designs that are key to our survival. We are now also starting to see research to support the same idea in the workplace.

Jasmine Hu from the University of Notre Dame's Mendoza College of Business considered the effects of team members working for the benefit of others[40]. Studying 67 different teams from six organisations in the US and China, Hu found that, "the greater the motivation to benefit others, the higher the levels of cooperation and viability and the higher the subsequent team performance".
Creating team players who are motivated to support and encourage other team members leads to the highest levels of team effectiveness, the researchers found. Helping others has positive implications not just for the individuals concerned, but also for the wider business. Creating a community of employees who feel like they are part of something might be the one thing that unites them, and this will sit at the centre of an organisation's culture.

Part of our Ikigai is a belief in the company we work for and what it's trying to achieve. Apple is a notable example of an organisation that does this. Despite paying their retail employees less than $25,000 a year, Apple has managed to get its staff to really buy into the company mission. In an interview with Fast Company, Retail Chief Angela Ahrendts states that money isn't ultimately the deciding factor when an employee comes to work for Apple[41]. Ahrendts said that Apple employees feel connected to something bigger. She told Fast Company, "[Apple] was built to change people's lives. That foundation, that service mentality, that drive to continue to change lives - that is a core value in the company".

In the 1980s when Steve Jobs was CEO, Apple's mission statement was; 'To make a contribution to the world by making tools for the mind that advance humankind'. A nice perk of a job at Apple is that employees get good discounts on Apple products[42]. Being users of Apple products is a key component to buying into the company's values and mission, because they're not just employees, they're consumers of Apple too. This helps employees to see and feel how the products they help to build and sell can help people enrich their lives.

Organisational values may be of importance to employers, but very few employees believe in them. Gallup report that less than 27 per cent of US employees believe in their company's values[43]. Outlining values that employees can identify with is the first part of the challenge. The values should then be made so clear that every employee can easily understand how their job and their daily tasks can contribute to the company.

Like Apple, Twitter has a famously simple mission statement: 'To give everyone the power to create and share ideas and information instantly, without barriers'. Company values are becoming so important to organisational culture, employees are actively seeking out those values that they can relate to. For employers, this means they end up recruiting employees that exactly fit the culture they want to cultivate, and that benefits everyone.

Interestingly, research shows there are negative effects to employees who work for organisation but don't fully buy into, or fake belief in, their employer's values. Published in Marginalia Online, associate Professor Patricia Hewlin found that it is common for employees to fake belief in organisational values[44]. However, Hewlin also found that those employees who supress their own values hinder their own careers.

Facebook spent a lot of time considering their company values, and ultimately came up with one of the most concise, easy-to-understand sets I've ever seen:

- Focus on impact
- Move fast
- Be bold
- Be open
- Build social value

When we consider what we know is important to an employee - encouraging them to be bold with their ideas, open with their colleagues, and to make an impact on society - Facebook have done a respectable job. Having a sense of purpose at work is something employees are finding increasingly important. We're also starting to see some surprising side effects to having a purpose at work, such as less insomnia and better-quality sleep.

We'll find out later in this book how important sleep is to employees, but how can having a sense of purpose lead to less sleep disturbances? Typically, our quality of sleep deteriorates as we get older, so researchers in this area have focused on older people. Researchers at Northwest University asked more than 800 older participants to complete a 32-item questionnaire assessing their sleep quality and symptoms of Restless Leg Syndrome and Sleep Apnoea[45]. They also measured their purpose in life using Ryff and Keye's scales of Psychological Wellbeing. They discovered that sleep disorders were lower among those people who measured high on having a purpose in life. Even in follow-up studies on the same participants one and two years later, the results remained the same.

By working for an organisation that encourages social good and has clear organisational values, employees can go a long way to achieving the kind of Ikigai most of us strive for, and more importantly, they could even improve their own mental health. In their book, Beyond Performance: How Great Organizations Build Ultimate Competitive Advantage, Scott Keller and Colin Prince say that giving their employees a sense of meaning in their work is critical to building a healthy, competitive organisation.

4. Meriggiare

Italy

If like me, you love food (especially Italian food) you'll enjoy this chapter. Meriggiare has no direct English translation, but in Italian, it means, "to escape the heat of the midday sun and seek shelter in the shade". For many of us, taking a lunchbreak at work can be a welcome escape from a stressful day, and for the Italians, it's a great excuse to indulge in their well-known love of food. It's estimated that the average workday lunch break in Italy lasts for more than an hour and frequently includes three courses.[46]

A 2011 survey by Birra Moretti[47] found that 100 per cent of Italian employees take lunch every single day, with 79 per cent leaving the office to do so. So many Italian employees leave work for long lunch breaks, that Government minister Gianfranco Rotondi said that the practice, "brings the country to a standstill" and called for a ban on the long lunch break to improve employee productivity. Nutritional Therapist and Workplace Wellbeing Specialist Joanne Crovini told me, "this kind of relaxed lunch not only provides you with a much-needed mental break from work but also means you will digest your food better. Meals eaten when feeling stressed or rushing from one place to another will contribute to bloating, wind and discomfort, whereas meals eaten slowly whilst relaxed will be better digested and the nutrients better absorbed".

In the UK, just one in five employees take the full traditional hour-long lunch break with the majority taking just 30 minutes or less[48]. New research even suggests that a third of employees admit to never leaving their desk or work station after they've arrived in the morning[49]. So, should the Italian Government be encouraging or restricting long lunch breaks? We've already learned from the Swedish and the Finnish of the benefits of taking a break from work. Taking short breaks from work is a proven way to improve concentration and energy for better productivity. But what about a longer, regular break at the middle of the working day?

One thing the Italians might have found out is that a long lunch break gives us time to think. Just like a computer, our minds need to be switched off and switched on again to be able to work properly. As we've already learned, mindfulness is a popular way for people to take their minds off the stresses of everyday life. Many employees now use their lunch break as an opportunity to meditate and take stock.

The Oxford Centre for Mindfulness has found that mindfulness prevents depression in those who have previously experienced three or four periods of recurrent depression by 30 to 40 per cent[50]. Ry Morgan, Co-Founder and CPO at Unmind agrees; "Mindfulness is a key a part of preventative mental health care and, alongside CBT and positive psychology, can be applied within the workplace to great effect.

Forward thinking organisations such as Google, Patagonia, GE and many others have been offering mindfulness training to staff for years – with incredible quantitative and qualitative results".

Research has found that people report less anxiety and depression after using mindfulness for just eight weeks[51]. Mindfulness has also shown to decrease stress, anxiety and fatigue, so its encouragement during the working day can be of huge benefit to employees. Crovini says that, "being mindful whilst eating also has huge benefits as, amongst other things, we are less likely to overeat, so step away from your screen for lunch".

Taking a regular lunchbreak and using this time to switch off from work can benefit employee mental health and wellbeing, but can it improve their work? Baylor University's Hankamer School of Business in Waco, Texas studied how taking a break from work makes employees perform better[52]. The researchers found that the more hours an employee worked before taking a break, the more the symptoms of poor health appeared, and the less energised employees felt. The researchers also found that working all morning and taking a late lunch is not as restorative as taking an early lunch. Over a long career as a Nutritional Therapist, Crovini says she has seen an increase in clients who are signed off work due to stress and are coming to see her to get themselves well before returning to work.

Crovini adds, "investing in employee wellbeing and encouraging a culture where staff take lunch breaks can decrease the incidence of long term leave due to stress". Time away from work in the middle of the day allows us to detach from work.

This mental and physical detachment has been shown to increase an employee's positive mood and satisfaction, as well as decreasing their chances of burnout[53]. Conversely, working through break times has a negative effect on employees. Those employees who work through their lunch breaks have been found to have decreased wellbeing, poorer sleep quality and an increase in negative mood[54]. Interestingly, taking regular breaks and ensuring we take a lunch break won't give us less time to do our jobs either. Research by social networking company the Draugiem Group[55], showed that their top 10 per cent most productive employees didn't put in any longer hours than anyone else in the company. In addition, The Muse also reports that their top 10 per cent of most productive employees take regular breaks[56].

Taking a lunch break is not just about having time away from work. Food literally fuels us and gives us the energy we need to be able to function properly. Researchers have conducted many studies into how food affects our cognitive performance and how carbohydrates can improve it[57]. Randall Kaplan et al discovered that energy intake from protein, carbohydrates or fat can enhance our memory and exert unique effects on cognition.

That lunchtime sandwich is more than just a chance to get away from your desk, it's helping to improve the quality of our work later in the day. Leigh Gibson from the University of Roehampton told Live Science that when our glucose levels drop, we get confused[58]. Crovini highlights, "our brain uses up to 40 per cent of the carbohydrate that we eat to function properly, meaning that without the right food at the right times we will struggle to concentrate". Crovini says, "the right fats are also essential for brain health and employees should eat plenty of oily fish, nuts, seeds and olive oil". With so many employees skipping a lunch break, researchers have started to look at the physical effects this might be having on their bodies.

Researchers from the National Institute on Aging looked at a sample of healthy men and women in their 40s[59]. They monitored them as they ate three meals a day for two months and then again when they ate only two meals, but their evening meal contained the same calories as two meals. The researchers found that skipping lunch and eating a larger meal in the evening produced risky metabolic changes, which could lead to diabetes. Additionally, those employees who skip lunch report it makes them feel ill at work and puts them in a bad mood for the rest of the day[60]. Crovini told me that when employees skip meals, they are more likely to eat sugary snacks and coffee, which negatively affect their blood sugar and therefore energy levels, leading to low mood and even anxiety.

Recently, David Leonhardt from The New York Times told readers that if they were feeling the pressure at work, they need to take a 'Shultz Hour'[61]. George Shultz was the Secretary of State during the 1980s, and he told The New York Times that he would set aside an hour every week for quiet reflection. Unless his wife or the President called, he was not to be disturbed. In a recent interview, Shultz told Leonhardt that this hour of alone time was his opportunity to think about the strategic aspects of his job. Known as 'task-negative mode', this practice gives us time away from work, and can create some of our greatest innovations.

The shower has become synonymous with great ideas, and for good reason. Research suggests that 72 per cent of people get their best ideas while showering[62]. The reason for this isn't the act of showering itself, but that this is a time when we are on our own, without the distractions of others or technology. Our focus is purely on the one, monotonous task of getting ourselves clean. Psychological Science Magazine[63] examined the cognitive processes underlying the situations when we let our minds wander. Researchers asked participants to perform an Unusual Use Task (UUT) by listing as many unusual uses for an item as they could. The participants were then asked to complete a demanding or an undemanding task, with one group being given a break, and another no break at all. Of all the groups, only those who performed the undemanding task improved their score on a second UUT test. The researchers concluded that simple tasks allow the mind to wander and may increase creative problem solving.

When we stop focusing on a task, we engage a part of the brain called the default mode network, or DMN. Our DMN uses a lot of our body's energy, even though it's not supposed to be doing anything. This resting network is operating under our consciousness by thinking of the past, the future, reliving old memories, and coming up with innovative ideas. For us to be able to tap into this network, we must give our minds time to rest. Putting our mind to rest activates this network, helping us to solve problems and be more creative without even knowing it[64].

For many employees, taking a lunchbreak gets them to stand up and move around. Technology in the modern office means employees are sedentary more than ever, and it's really damaging their health. A 2017 study published in the Annals of Internal Medicine looked at correlations between middle-aged Americans' sitting habits and their mortality[65]. Researchers discovered that the length of time someone sits, and the frequency of how often they sit down, might be a predictor of risk of death. Researchers suggest that employees should have some standing movement every 30 minutes and increase regular exercise to combat the effects of our sitting.

In 2012, the athletics company New Balance piloted a scheme called 'Organisations in Motion' with Wellness and Prevention, Inc[66]. The scheme was created to measure the impact of frequent, short increases in physical activity throughout the working day. More than 700 employees at the company's Boston office took part.

By the end of the pilot, 53 per cent of employees said they had increased their levels of daily activity and 89 per cent said they planned to continue to do so. The increase in physical activity at work led to almost half of employees reporting to have higher energy levels and engagement at work. The additional activity also appeared to improve employee perceptions of their work, as measures around how inspiring employees found their jobs and how enthusiastic they were increased. Clearly, taking time away from our work commitments and the pressure of the workplace can aid our wellbeing.

A 2013 study by the University of Queensland found that when employees took their lunch break at a restaurant with colleagues or friends, they reported feeling more relaxed than those who stayed in the office on their own[67]. Allowing ourselves to take a lunchbreak from work gives us the perfect opportunity to let our minds and legs wander. Letting our minds relax isn't always about being idle.

Research shows that while mind wandering takes place, the brain is still very active[68]. Interestingly, neural recruitment is strongest when we are unaware of our own mind wandering. This suggests that we can't force our minds to wander, we must put ourselves in situations that naturally allow us to do this, and a lunch break from work might be the ideal time to encourage this wandering.

5. Geborgenheit

Germany

Geborgenheit (pronounced Ger-bor-gen-heit) has no direct translation from German, but generally refers to a feeling of security and wellbeing. In a workplace context, this has become important to employees as a basis for creating a positive culture (one of the key factors that improves the employee experience).

In 2016, it was reported that there was a problem with Germany's employee engagement[69]. In Gallup's State of the Workplace report, just 16 per cent of German employees were engaged with their jobs. This means a massive 68 per cent were disengaged and didn't have any passion or energy for their work. Analysis of low engagement in Germany has started to point at managers and the culture they create as a starting point of the problem. In Gallup's report, just seven per cent of engaged employees have thought about leaving their current job due to their direct line manager, compared to a massive 48 per cent of disengaged employees.

Gallup report that a quarter of employees have left a job in the past just to get away from a bad manager. Organisations must realise that for many employees, managers set the tone. There is no point having a set of values and cornerstones if the management team don't live these values every day. The best managers lead by example, are great communicators, and work collaboratively with their teams.

Attracting and retaining the right kind of people that will become your managers of the future is a good place to start tackling the problem of disengagement.

In the book What People Want: A Manager's Guide to Building Relationships That Work, the author Terry Bacon describes the elements every employee wants to see in their manager. Employees want managers who are trustworthy, dependable, honest and collaborative. They also want to feel listened to, and want their interactions with their manager to feel genuine. French President Emmanuel Macron recently told Der Speigel that the only way we can move forward is if we do this together[70]. Macron said, "the goal I have set myself: To try to encourage France and the French people to change and develop further. But that can only be done as a collective, with one another. You have to bundle the strength of those who want to take that step". Macron realises that it's a collective group that progresses things, and managers also need to realise that they don't make positive change on their own. Making employees feel like they are part of a culture that makes them feel secure isn't just about looking after employees, it's also about looking after profits. We've already seen how highly employees value trust in their management team, but it needs to go further. Employees need to feel that their managers care about their teams.

In their global study, Gallup also ask employees what kinds of things make them move onto other roles[71]. It's not money; only 22 per cent of employees surveyed said they left their job for more money.

Discussing the results, Gallup's Chief Scientist for Workplace Management, James K. Harter, Ph.D., says, "at least 75 per cent of the reasons for voluntary turnover can be influenced by managers. Still, many bosses think… that all turnover comes down to money". More than 15 per cent of employees left jobs directly as a result of their manager, but clearly managers can actually be doing a lot more to encourage employees to stay and develop.

For most employees, their line manager is their primary point of contact with those who run the organisation. Ensuring the management team is on board with our organisational culture will be key to its success. In the UK, the public shaming of poor management by employers like Sports Direct has gained significant media attention. Line managers have been reported to be reading the results of employee surveys that were supposed to be anonymous. This has led to employees being fearful for their jobs and distrusting their management team as employee names were linked to survey results[72].

Even more recently, the questionable working practices and unfair treatment of employees at Uber resulted in their licence being revoked by Transport for London. Transport for London cited 'lack of corporate social responsibility' for the shock move that will cost Uber tens of millions in lost revenue.

The event trigged a companywide email from Uber CEO Dara Khosrowshahi in which he said, "the truth is that there is an excessive cost to a bad reputation… it really matters what people think of us, especially in a global business like ours, where actions in one part of the world can have serious consequences in another"[73].

Right across the world, companies are being called out for their poor attitude to their employees; from the Barclays libor scandal to sales practices at Wells Fargo. This has all led to significant changes in the working cultures of other brands conscious of not falling into the same trap. Whirlpool Corp and Citigroup are two organisations that are making sure their employees are comfortable reporting bad practices[74]. This highlights a growing trend in responsible and emotionally intelligent employers. A new study released earlier this year revealed that employers who care about their employees report higher profits than those who don't. Of those top 100 best companies to work for, for almost 20 years the companies on the list have outperformed the S&P 500 stock index by a ratio of almost two to one[75]. A little less cut throat and a little more arm around shoulder is the latest trend in achieving higher growth.

The research from consulting firm Great Place to Work has found that the strongest driver of above average revenue growth among smaller businesses is a caring community at work[76]. Employees identified 'caring' as more pivotal for business growth than having clear strategies, innovation and competent leaders.

The research looked at several hundred small and medium-sized organisations, and examined more than 52,000 employee surveys. The authors tried to find out the strongest drivers of increased revenue by looking at the impact of around 60 questions from Great Place to Work's Trust Index Survey. They discovered that employees are 44 per cent more likely to work for a company with above average growth when they feel like they are being cared for.

The links between being a caring employer and overall business success compare with previous research in this area. Fortune online describes how Google recently learned that psychological safety is the primary influence in what fuels high performance.[77] Some of the world's largest organisations realise the importance of asking questions and listening to your employees' concerns. Satya Nadella, CEO of Microsoft once said, "listen to your customers and your employees - they are the most important thing and define your business".

Psychological safety is the belief that people feel safe taking risks and making mistakes without fear of negative consequences. In early 2017, the Coca-Cola Company welcomed James Quincey as their new Chief Executive. In one of his first interviews as the new CEO, Quincey shared one piece of advice with his staff: "Make mistakes". The very essence of psychological safety is that team members will be more innovative and happy at work if they feel like they can make mistakes and learn from them.

Without the ability to speak up and take risks, some of the world's best ideas would never have come to fruition. A 2010 Chinese study looked at members and leaders of more than 100 diverse groups in Shanghai[78]. They found that psychological safety can be shaped by leaders, and in turn its development induces learning within a team.

Who an employer chooses as their management is hugely important to how employees will feel towards them, and ultimately the organisation. The adage, "people don't leave jobs, they leave managers" is true in many cases. A Gallup study of more than 7,000 global employees found that half of all US employees have left a job because of the boss they had to work for[79]. The report also revealed that only 35 per cent of US managers were engaged themselves. As we learnt from Germany, it is near impossible for a manager to inspire and support their team if they aren't engaged themselves.

The UK Advisory, Conciliation and Arbitration Service (ACAS) recommends for organisations to thrive, it's up to line managers to relate to their staff[80]. Training line managers to develop emotional intelligence skills and other 'soft skills' is key to creating a good employee experience. If managers don't care, how can we expect them to create a safe and comfortable environment for their employees? Especially given that how we feel about our jobs can have a significant effect on how we feel about our whole lives.

In a now famous interview, Chief Executive Officer of PepsiCo Australia and New Zealand, Robbert Rietbroek, told news.com.au that he asks all his managers to, "leave loudly"[81]. Rietbroek says that for all employees to feel comfortable leaving work earlier to pick their kids up from school or attend an appointment, they need to see that the management team do that too. Rietbroek explained, "so for instance, if I occasionally go at 4pm to pick up my daughters, I will make sure I tell the people around me, 'I'm going to pick up my children.' Because if it's okay for the boss, then it's okay for middle management and new hires." The culture of PepsiCo has allowed employees to be openly flexible at work, and that builds trust with their management. PepsiCo has managed to reduce its turnover by 12 per cent and kept hold of their best talent for longer.

In Robert Lavingna's book Engaging Government Employees, the author recalls how Gallup researchers identified what factors contribute to employee wellbeing. Aside from social, financial and physical wellbeing, the researchers also found that career wellbeing might be a principal element of an employee's overall wellbeing. Other research states there is a positive relationship between an employee's engagement at work and their overall wellbeing outside of work too[82]. If an employee's Geborgenheit isn't being satisfied at work or by their manager, it can have much wider implications outside of work, and so it's very important to both employee and employer that we get it right.

Humans strive for a sense of community and belonging, so it's no surprise that employees want the same from their employment. Life is difficult and there are some serious factors outside of work that have a massive impact on our lives. The loss of loved ones, financial difficulty, childcare and eldercare are all big emotional issues that are bound to have an impact on an employee's ability to do their job. However, when a manager understands this, accommodates and cares for their employee's needs, the results are quite surprising. As we've already seen, the Fortune 100 reveals a lot about being a good employer. Companies with higher employee happiness and engagement show much higher than average performance.

For example, those companies on the Fortune 100 that have moved to a flexible work model to help employees accommodate their lives outside of work, report productivity increases of anywhere between 30 per cent and a staggering 60 per cent[83].

In the book Make More Money by Making Your Employees Happy, Dr Noelle Nelson explains how organisations can increase profits by caring for employees' needs. When Paul O'Neil became CEO of the world's leading producer of aluminium, Aloca, he announced that his sole priority was to increase the safety of his employees. Although not well received by his board, he understood that safety was a big concern for employees. Over the next 13 years employee productivity increased as accident rates decreased dramatically, with some plants going years without any accidents at all.

When Paul O'Neil left Aloca 10 years later, their annual income had grown by more than 500 per cent.

Caring for employees is no longer just the right thing to do, it makes clear business sense. Caring and compassionate employers might appear to be rare in the world, but Jane Dutton believes investment in compassion will eventually pay off[84]. For more than six years, Dutton - from the University of Michigan - studied an array of organisational settings, from hospitals and universities, to large global businesses like Cisco. She found that when employees are given emotional support by their employer, they display more positive emotions and a higher commitment to the organisation.

In a famous email published by Electrek[85], Tesla CEO Elon Musk told all his employees, "no words can express how much I care about your safety and wellbeing". Musk told every employee that any accident will get reported straight to him and he will meet with the safety team weekly. He also promised to meet every injured person to better understand what went wrong, and make sure it never happens again. This unprecedented message from a well-known CEO sent a very strong signal to employers everywhere; if we don't care for our employees, someone else will.

The interesting thing about compassion and caring at work is that it means the most when it comes from leadership. To foster a culture of compassion, we need to start with our management team.

In her research, Dutton quotes the work of Melwani et al who revealed that people who act compassionately are perceived more strongly as leaders. In my experience, having a caring boss is like the golden ticket of employment - if you ever find that, keep hold of it for as long as you can.

6. Arbetsdag

Sweden

In a widely-publicised move, Sweden trialed a reduced arbetsdag in 2015. Meaning 'working day', it was the subject of a two-year study that looked at the impact of reducing it to just six hours[86]. The study revealed that employees reported feeling healthier, and absence rates were reduced by shortening the working day. The initial aim of the pilot was to get more done in less time and allow employees to spend more time with their families outside of work.

One of the companies participating in the Swedish study saw around 68 nurses at a care home have their working day cut to six hours to improve staff morale and patient care. The results were very surprising. The care home employees reported being 20 per cent happier, and had more energy. This extra energy allowed them to do 64 per cent more activities with residents, (the metric used to measure their productivity). Although these results showed the trial achieved all its goals, it came at a cost. Bloomberg reported in early 2017[87] that it cost the employer around £1.4m in additional funding. This was needed to employ more staff to cover the lessened hours. As a result, they decided not to make the working hours reduction permanent. However, some Swedish employers who made the change many years ago have stuck with it. In Gothenburg, Toyota moved to a six-hour working day 13 years ago.

Since making the change, they have reported happier employees, lower staff turnover and even an increase in profits. More importantly, they've never looked back. This new way of working has enticed many new employees to work for Toyota.

However, Sweden wasn't the first country to pose the theory that a shorter working day would benefit both employers and employees. In 2014, The Productivity of Working Hours was published by John Pencavel for the Institute for the Study of Labor[88]. The researchers of this study collected vast amounts of data from those working in munitions during the First World War. The study found that there was a non-linear relationship between working hours and employee productivity. Pencavel concluded that working days need to be shorter. They found that output from workers reduced once 48 hours had been hit. When an employee worked 70 hours or more, their output was pretty much the same as when they completed 56 hours. The extra 14 hours made no difference to their productivity, and was like it hadn't been worked at all.

In 2017, the world turned its attention back to Sweden as many thought leaders believed the longer-term savings weren't considered in the original study. As reported in Bloomberg, the long-term effects of the shorter working day were quite surprising. The care home nurses in Gothenburg reported fewer sick days and even more sleep than when their days were longer. They also took fewer average sick days than nurses across the entire city of Gothenburg.

The long-term health benefits for employees working shorter days will have inevitable impacts on the economics of running a business. According to the report Sickness Absence in the Nordic Countries[89], long term sickness is very high in Norway and Sweden. Almost 30 per cent of Swedish workers report taking health related leave during 2014. Unauthorised absence is a big cost to Swedish employers and any strategy aimed at reducing this can levy large financial savings.

Even if employers aren't willing or able to commit to reducing the working day significantly, there appear to be benefits to any reduction in the traditional eight hour working day. According to a poll by YouGov, most employees believe a working day of seven hours or less would see them be more productive[90]. Almost half of all employees in the UK believe the working week should be less than five days. Almost three quarters of UK employees believe a shorter working week would improve the happiness of the nation. The feeling towards this is so strong that almost a third of employees would give up a day's pay to be able to work one day less a week[91]. There is clearly a demand to change the rules of working times we've all stuck with for so long.

We've lived with the eight-hour working day for over 100 years and although many believe shortening it is the way forward, there are some who believe cutting it almost in half is the only way to get tangible results.

In his book The Five Hour Workday, author Stephen Aarstol outlines how he cut his employees' workday to just five hours.

Aarstol believes that we are kidding ourselves if we think our employees are really doing eight hours or more of work a day. He believes most employees are only productive for two to three hours a day. Shortening the working day and focusing on making employees more productive was his goal when he trialled a five-hour working day at his company in 2015. So successful was it, that he implemented the five-hour working day permanently. The results were very surprising. By 2016 Aarstol's San Diego organisation was named a fastest-growing company, and in 2016 his nine-person team generated more than $9 million in revenue. Allowing employees to work from 8am to 1pm means they can use their afternoons to do what's important to them outside of work. Employees return to work the next day feeling relaxed and refreshed, ready for an intensive five-hour shift.

When we consider our own working day, we will all be familiar with the usual distractions that impede on our productivity. For me, I used to love going to the office early, before the phones starting ringing and before people could interrupt my work. I used to get my best work done first thing in the morning or during overtime when everyone had left the office. A shorter working day would enable employees to schedule more appointments in their own time, reduce the costs of childcare, and more importantly, give them more time off work. We'll find out later in this book why that is so important.

According to Forbes, 44 per cent of US female doctors now work four or less days a week.

A shorter working day has obvious benefits to mothers and fathers. Increased and shared parental leave have started a trend that sees the workplace more understanding of family life than perhaps ever before. Reducing the working day for parents gives them valuable time to spend with their children. It's an all too familiar story of the parent arriving home after the children have gone to bed. This extra family time can have significant emotional benefits to all involved.

The reduction of the working day is as much about ensuring employees don't work longer hours as it is making their days shorter. Published in the American Journal of Epidemiology, a 2009 study looked at the effects of working long hours on employees of middle age[92]. More than 2,000 full-time British civil servants were studied. Those employees working more than 11 hours a day (compared with those working eight) scored lower in vocabulary and reasoning tests. I don't believe we are built to be working as much as we do currently.

As technology dramatically changes how and where we work, home working has become an extremely popular benefit. Home working gives employees the chance to avoid long, stressful commutes and the distractions that are common at work. For many employees, the commute delivers the perfect storm of annoyance and frustration that means they start the day in a negative mood.

Research from the University of the West of England found that a slight increase of just 20 minutes to an employee's commute is as bad as getting a 19 per cent pay cut[93].

Giving employees the chance to stay 'on the clock', but leave the office earlier or even work from home a few days a week, might be an alternative solution to a shortening the working day. In his now famous TED Talk, Stanford Professor of Economics Nicholas Bloom talks about a company in Singapore which forced half of its workforce to work from home for four days a week.

Bloom reveals that the two-year-long study showed a massive increase in productivity – equal to an extra working day. This research also revealed that those employees who worked from home were more likely to be retained by the employer than those who didn't. The removal of a commute saved time for both the employer and employee. In an ACAS research paper[94], Alexandra Beauregard, Kelly Basile and Esther Canonico studied the benefits of homeworking. They found that those employees who worked from home reported higher job satisfaction and engagement. They also found that home working (and even partial home working) are linked with significantly lower levels of work-related stress.

A reduction in the working day isn't a radical, new idea. The idea of an eight-hour working day was created because of the hours of daylight and the running of 24-hour factories.

As our society has evolved, these working hours should really have evolved with it, but we've seen no changes in more than 100 years. In 1926, Henry Ford reduced the working week for his employees from six to five days and he didn't cut wages. He assumed that his employees' productivity would increase, and he was right. If we want to get the best out of our employees, it's important that every employee can create a decent work-life balance that works for them.

Technology has meant that the traditional lines between working hours are blurred, and so it's never been more important to create those boundaries so that your work life doesn't affect your home life, and vice versa. The diagram below illustrates what a delicate balance this can be for employees.

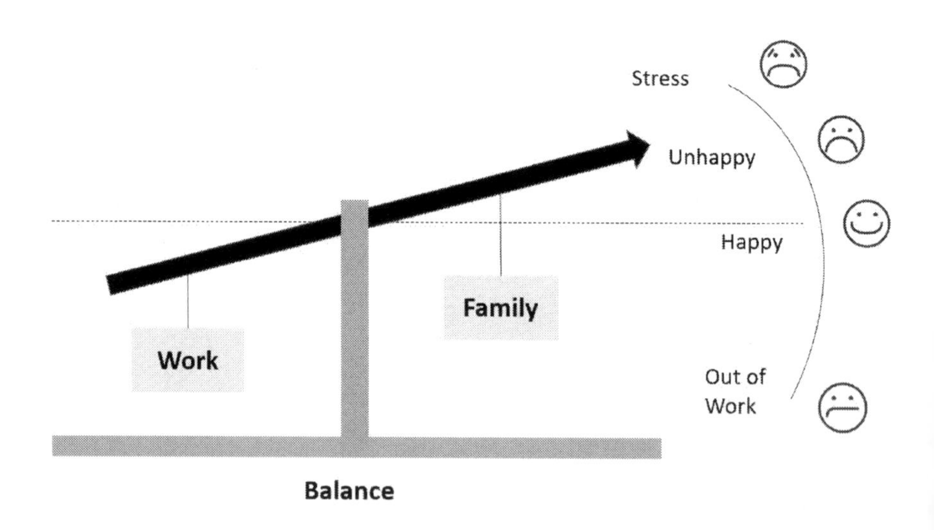

Flexible working patterns are now so important to certain generations that those who are caught between looking after their kids and ageing parents are referred to as 'The Sandwich Generation'. One in eight Americans in their 40s and 50s has a parent aged 65 years or older, while also raising a child[95]. Almost half of Americans caring for their parents' state that their careers have suffered[96], so, for these types of employees, even a minor change to their working pattern can have a positive effect.

We'll learn more about the importance of accommodating your employees' care responsibilities later in this book. Empowering and trusting employees to fit work around their family commitments creates vast amounts of positivity between the employer and employee.

But it's not just those employees who have care responsibilities outside of work says Samantha Gee, Former HR Direct and Reward Specialist and Founder of Verditer Consulting. "It's an amazing opportunity to give time, thought and energy to things that are important to an employee personally outside of work. Work doesn't have to fall into 'packages' of 35/40 hours each week! I think it would help if employers saw the power of enabling flexible working whatever the reason e.g. pursuing other interests such as travel, starting a business, learning a skill, or just getting fitter and healthier". The traditional model of an eight-hour working day is fast becoming old news.

As flexible working frequently tops employees' lists of 'must haves', and as more employees work remotely, employees are now being measured by their output, rather than hours worked.

7. Siesta

Spain

For some lucky employees, there are parts of the world where napping during the day has become commonplace. We are all familiar with the Spanish siesta, taken from the Spanish word for 'nap'. Usually taken in the early afternoon, the tradition is popular in many Hispanic countries, or those where the climate is particularly warm. But is there any proof that a siesta has benefits in the workplace? Well yes, and quite a lot. As we'll discover later in this book, any workplace practice that helps improve an employee's sleep deprivation should be welcomed. Sleep deprivation has been linked with some serious health conditions such as depression, diabetes and obesity.

In fact, so debilitating is lack of sleep, that it has been used as one of the CIA's most popular methods of torture because of the psychological impacts it has on human beings[97]. But encouraging employees to get more sleep makes business sense. Sleep-deprived employees are costing the UK economy £40bn a year[98]. In Japan, 600,000 days are lost in productivity due to sleep deprivation alone. The effects of sleep deprivation in the workplace are so serious that new research has shown moderate deprivation is as equivalent to being drunk[99].

Published in Occupational and Environmental Medicine, researchers examined how performance was affected when participants were subjected to sleep deprivation over a period of 28 hours, and then again after receiving a dose of alcohol. The researchers concluded that the fatigue of sleep deprivation was a factor in the inferior performance (speed and accuracy) of the kind needed to be safe on the road, or in industrial settings. Would you allow a drunk employee to interact with customers? Probably not…

The impact of sleep deprivation in society is having huge negative effects. In one study, published in the Journal of Psychological Science, researchers looked at the impact sleep deprivation had on American criminal judges. In results that gained wide media attention and shocked those working in crime and punishment, the researchers found that the degree of punishment handed out to criminals was affected by the amount of sleep the judge had the night before. In U.S. Federal Courts, it was revealed that judges handed out longer sentences when they were sleep deprived[100].

Sleep deprivation can also affect an employee's lateral thinking and ability to be innovative[101]. According to the US Chamber Foundation, innovation is the key driver to economic growth and overall business success[102]. Just one poor night's sleep can cause enough impairment in employees to affect their innovation. To explore this theory, Harrison and Horne adapted a marketing decision-making game to measure participants' performances[103].

The task relied on participants understanding substantial amounts of text and performing a critical reasoning test. Participants were tested with and without sleep, and the researchers discovered that performance in the game deteriorated significantly after 32 to 36 hours of sleep loss. An increase in errors and lack of understanding of the text was attributed to sleep loss.

It is widely believed that the best amount of sleep for adults is seven to nine hours a day. However, studies have shown that a third of adults get only six hours - which leads to sleep deprivation[104]. With an average working day of around eight and a half hours, that leaves just six and a half hours a day for getting ready for work, commuting and the evening's entertainment. It's not surprising that many employees are pushing back their bedtime in exchange for leisure pursuits or more time at work[105]. But can employers really help? Many believe that employers are restricted by what they can do to help employees with sleep deprivation. However, there is a growing trend to allow employees to sleep at work. Arianna Huffington, editor of The Huffington Post and author of the book The Sleep Revolution, says if they don't have designated nap rooms in their office, employers should consider placing couches in a private spot for taking naps. That's how serious some experts believe the situation is.

According to advice from the National Sleep Foundation in the US, "a short nap of 20 to 30 minutes can help to improve mood, alertness and performance".

Although new to some of us, the trend to offer sleeping areas in the workplace is growing significantly in the USA. Organisations like The Huffington Post and Google have become well known for their 'NapQuest' rooms and 'Energy Pods', and nap rooms have been implemented by other organisations like Ben and Jerry's and Uber. Could the future of work see nap rooms commonplace?

Spain isn't the only country synonymous with afternoon napping. Argentinian workplaces have been embracing afternoon naps for almost 10 years. Argentinian organisations like the University of Buenos Aires have designated napping spaces for employees who are feeling tired throughout the day. The reason behind this cultural change might be because Argentina ranks as being an especially sleep-deprived country. It was ranked third in the world on a list of countries struggling to get enough sleep. World Crunch reports that 15 per cent of Argentinians sleep less than six hours a night[106]. That's seven million people – equivalent of the entire population of London – that are being sleep-deprived in Argentina every day.

In the Journal of Personality and Individual Differences[107], psychologists showed that napping can increase positive mood and improve immune functioning. Their study also discovered that the napping participants could tolerate frustration significantly longer than non-nappers. The benefits to building and maintaining good working relationships could be much improved if we were able to reduce the negative effects of employee frustration. The study also found that participants were less impulsive after a 60-minute nap.

These results indicate that emotional control may become impaired from growing tired, and that napping may be an effective countermeasure.

According to an employee benefits survey of 600 American companies conducted by the Society for Human Resource Management[108], six per cent of workplaces had nap rooms in 2011, a slight increase from five per cent the previous year. Even more compelling, a 2011 poll of 1,500 adults by the National Sleep Foundation[109] found that 34 per cent of respondents say their employers allow them to nap at work, and 16 per cent said their employers also have designated napping areas.

There has been so much research into the area of sleep over the past few years, that TIME Magazine has referred to quality sleep as, "the fountain of youth". Mark Zielinski is an associate faculty member in Behavioral Neuroscience at Harvard Medical School. He recently noticed that his lab mice slept in cycles of 12 hours[110]. This prompted him to adjust their sleep cycle by leaving the lab lights on, so they'd stay awake longer than usual. He'd also shake their cages to keep them from dropping off. As he did this, he noticed they displayed all the characteristics of being tired: drooping eyelids and low brain activity. However, he also noticed that after this disturbance, even after he left them alone to go to sleep, they didn't. He found that once disturbed, their sleep quality wasn't the same as it had been before. They weren't getting as much deep sleep as they needed.

Once their sleep had been disturbed, Zielinksi suspected that the mice were missing the signals from their brains that told their body's it was time to go to sleep,

We all know how we feel waking up early compared to how we feel after a superior quality night's sleep. So, it shouldn't really surprise any of us that we need the restorative power of sleep to function at our best. However, as more and more papers are published in this area, more psychologists are realising just how important sleep is to almost every function of the body. Matthew Walker, Professor of Neuroscience and Psychology at the University of California, Berkeley, told TIME Magazine in 2017 that, "sleep is the single most effective thing you can do to reset your brain and body for health"[111].

The sleep deprivation issue might be one of the most significant challenges to the workplace in the next 20 years. As employers start to accept some responsibility for the health of their staff, better sleep will emerge as the number one issue on HR's wellbeing agenda.

8. Guanxi

China

'Guanxi' is the name the Chinese give their personal networks of influence. It originates from old Chinese philosophy, and stresses the importance of relationships built around trust and reciprocity. Although quite a complex system, it basically refers to the relationships that we can call on for favours. It is common for Chinese people to grow an intricate web of guanxi relationships that last for extended periods of time. However, the key way to maintain these relationships is to return the favors that are given to us. Failure to reciprocate is considered an unforgivable offence.

The workplace is where these types of relationships can be of the most value. The culture of China means that people typically place a lot of importance on being able to respect and trust another person. Developing a good guanxi can result in better problem solving, quick responses to requests, and help when we need it. This kind of working together can have clear benefits to both employee and employer.

In the West, starting to build our own guanxi can be simple, as networking and social media is making this process easier and easier for employees. In China, an individual's guanxi can win or lose a business deal. A lot of time has been dedicated by sales professionals over the years to work out the best way to get that elusive sale.

We've all heard of the adage, "people buy from people", and it has some credibility in research.

The reason I've put guanxi in this book is that I've always felt that building relationships will add significant value to anyone's career progression. Networking is something that I think a lot of employees can benefit from, and it's never been easier to network than it is today. There are currently 467 million people across 200 countries on LinkedIn, with two new members joining every second in 2016. Professional networking has become the staple of the business world with many employees using sites like LinkedIn to find employment, as well as new business opportunities. Nick Court, Founder and CEO of Cloud9 People told me "networking should be high on everyone's agenda. Internally, it helps to drive understanding of the work your colleagues do, what your impact is on them, and theirs on you – how you can work better together".

Although there has been little research into the effects of networking on an employee's career, there was one significant study conducted in 2008. In their paper The Effects of Networking on Career Success, Hans-Georg and Klaus Moser discovered that networking was related to salary and salary growth over a period. Defined as 'building, maintaining and using relationships', networking was also seen by the researchers as having a positive effect on career success. This study found a direct correlation between participants who networked, and the speed of their salary progression over time.

They also discovered that those employees who engage in networking are more satisfied at work than those who don't[112]. Court adds, "humans are empathy-driven in the main, and only ever talking on the phone or over email means that people forget they are dealing with another person from time to time". Networking face to face builds emotional connections and creates a support network an employee can call upon in times of need. In the past, my own network has proven vital in finding a new job and even in writing this book.

Networking expert Deborah Mills-Scofield says that one of the biggest assets in someone's life is having a generous network. Mills-Scofield also says that our ability to network might be key to our survival. Writing in the Harvard Business Review[113], Mills-Scofield says that no matter how good we are, or our team at work is, we can't know everything. Networking allows us to learn about new things that can help us grow as individuals. I interviewed Samantha Gee, former HR Director and Reward Specialist, and Founder of Verditer Consulting about networking. Gee told me, "as the customer/client/competitor relationship becomes more complex and more diverse, the less we can assume we truly understand them. Companies are engaging increasingly in alliances, so organisations who were once competitors or clients may see opportunities to work together. It's therefore critical that we spend time with these groups in order to reflect them in how we work and what we deliver".

As well as improving our ability to do our jobs by making connections with similar professionals and expanding our knowledge, networking can also have positive effects our mental health by improving our self-esteem.

In 2010, researcher Susanne Ruehle, considered how guanxi can give people competitive advantage in times of economic crisis. Ruehle set out to prove that China's survival in times of economic stress was not down to the country, but down to its adoption of guanxi. The study found that certain features of guanxi helped individuals to survive these tough times in business. Guanxi gives individuals stability and security and is of most importance during times of economic instability[114].

In Sociology, the term 'dyad' was created to refer to a group of two people. Dyadic relationships are hugely important to employees' personal lives, but in a business context they could be just as important. The ESB Business School at Reutlingen University considered the importance of mutually beneficial relationships in the sports sponsorship dyad. Their research shows that there is a direct correlation between the most successful sporting sponsorship deals, and the relationship between the sports entity and its sponsor[115]. The relationship one person had with another was a large contributor to the success of the deal. As someone whose career was built on forging relationships, I believe that our business relationships are vital to organisational success.

Building relationships within your industry and with your peers and customers can pay huge dividends.

There is a widely publicised skills gap in the UK as employers struggle to get women into science, technology, engineering and maths (STEM) roles. This has sparked an interest into how women can use networking to aid career progression[116]. A study on the use of social networking found that women use LinkedIn significantly less than men[117]. Social networking could be of benefit to women seeking STEM roles. LinkedIn as a networking tool has grown massively since its inception in 2002, so its importance to networking will continue to grow. In 2017, more than 500 million users and 10 million job postings were listed on the social networking site. It's even claimed responsibility for aiding some significant and well-known investment deals. But where this kind of networking really helps employers is the ability to sell socially.

Social selling is an innovative approach to sales that utilises an employee's ability to network, and research shows that those who use it are outperforming those who don't. At the heart of social selling is the building of relationships by strategically placing ourselves into conversations online, at the right time. By using their online network, employees can advance their new business opportunities. Mark Fidelman, Social Sales Expert told Forbes[118] that, "selling through social channels is the closest thing to being a fly on the wall in your customer's, prospect's and competitor's world".

Not all the best employees will work with you. However, modern employers are starting to realise that their employees can benefit from 'open innovation'.

Open innovation is where employers encourage their employees to network with others, particularly those in research institutes, competitors and customers. Lots of research in this area is pointing to this kind of networking as being critical in an organisation's ability to innovate[119].

The Harvard Business Review conducted their own research into open innovation, and concluded that not enough employees were allocating enough time to using their external networks[120]. Organisations must allow employees to spend time on developing relationships with external partners, thereby enabling employees to cultivate these relationships to truly understand their market and provide benefits to their organisation.

In addition to those external networks we can build and maintain, employees should also focus on the same with their colleagues. Recently, researchers compiled and reviewed the evidence from 58 past workplace studies across 15 different countries. An analysis of the results showed that those people who identified more strongly with their colleagues displayed greater psychological wellbeing and better physical health than those who didn't.

The authors theorised that this ability to feel like, "we're all in this together" enables us to see the world through the perspective of a group, rather than just ourselves[121].

Our ability to build relationships in a business context opens us up to having a larger support network. This network can help employees learn more industry knowledge, keep up-to-date with market news, job search, and gather ideas. Spending more time with customers, colleagues and competitors means employees can give their employer the competitive advantage.

Developing their own guanxi can help them to remain close to customers, long after they have stopped being one. This means their relationships with them can remain stronger, and last longer.

9. Tillis

Denmark

In Denmark, employees appear to have more 'tillis' (or trust), than anywhere else in the world. Author of How to Live in Denmark, Kay Xander Mellish says, "trust is the basis of Danish society". Employees are expected to complete their work; when and where they get it done isn't important. This level of trust means employees can frequently work from home, or leave early. Working fewer hours and home working isn't affecting Danes' productivity. Employees in Denmark use the opportunity to get their heads down and work, to make the most of their lives outside of work. This has huge benefits to the work-life balance and consequently, Denmark has some of the highest employee satisfaction statistics in the world[122].

"The amount of trust is surprising. People leave the office to do things whenever they need to. Working hours are more flexible and colleagues and employers have confidence in each other, and trust that their work will be done adequately"[123], so says Marie Preisler from The Nordic Labour Journal. The Danish experience shows that trust-based leadership results in employees that are both happier and more engaged in their work. According to The Economist, just like Denmark, most Nordic countries not only have some of the highest levels of trust in the world, they also have high global competitiveness, human development, and prosperity[124].

One of the secrets of their success is their ability to be transparent with their people.

Jackie Buttery, former Global Head of Reward and Benefits at Herbert Smith Freehills, now and independent consultant, thinks trust is something we need. "We all want to feel like we are trusted to do a good job". Buttery believes that many HR policies and reward structures are about managing risk and delivering consistency. "You rarely see any reference to endangering trust in a line manager's performance objectives, and individuals are very often rewarded for individual success, rather than collective effort". Buttery thinks we need to be rewarding employees the 'how' as well as the 'what'. "We need to create reward structures that reward the effort and reward the experimentation that can transform the 'good' to 'great'. Trust is needed for that to happen".

Encouraging tillis in the workplace isn't just about creating trust, it's about removing distrust. Buttery says, "when organisations are smaller, the individual contributions are very obvious, and the working relationships are very close. As organisations get bigger, they can somehow lose their way, they can lose that closeness and become suspicious. Trust can then unravel".

In a study by Wharton at the University of Pennsylvania, researchers found that if trust gets harmed, it never fully recovers[125].

Managers and employers who lose the trust of their employees need to work extremely hard to regain it and even then, it will never be at the same level it once was. It's also important for employees to see trust in action. The way a manager acts and trusts employees will have an impact on the rest. If a manager loses the trust of just one employee and fails to get it back, this could be felt by other employees too. With the increasing reliance on technology at work, the 'human touch' is starting to disappear from management, and that can cause enormous amounts of distrust as employees talk to each other less and rely on technology to pass the message. The biggest culprit of this is email.

One of the biggest email taboos is the use of 'cc'ing' people (usually a manager) into an email. Even though employees may be doing this with the best of intentions, new research shows that doing so can create a culture of distrust in the workplace. The study by David De Cremer, KPMG Professor of Management Studies at Cambridge Judge Business School[126], looked at how copying a manager into an email influences an employee's attitude towards trust in their organisations. The researchers collected data from almost 1,000 people across the US, China, the Netherlands and UK. Unsurprisingly, they found that copying a manager into an email fostered, "a culture of fear and low psychological safety". The participants said that cc'ing the boss into an email signals that the sender does not trust their co-worker. They also found that the more often this happened, the less trusted the employees felt.

Building trust is something that can take years to achieve and just a moment to break. One of the most effective ways to build trust in the workplace is to build a personal connection with our colleagues. New research is showing that demonstrating our warmth contributes much more significantly to others' opinion of us than anything else.

Social psychologist at Princeton, Alex Todorov, has studied the cognition and neural mechanisms that drive the judgements we make about others[127]. His research shows that people pick up warmth as a quality quicker than anything else. Building trust requires a relationship based on an emotional connection, a management skill that (as we'll learn later in this book) will be in high demand in the future.

In 2017, the Edelman Trust Barometer revealed that, "trust is in crisis around the world". Looking at four key institutions including business, researchers have found that there has been a rapid decline in trust since they first started tracking it in 2002. If we look at leadership (specifically for CEOs), trust is at an all-time low for CEO credibility. Employees have rated their CEOs as not being credible in 23 out of 28 countries. Japan, France, Poland, South Korea, Canada, Australia and Hong Kong all rate as some of the lowest scorers. The UK and US have dropped by 12 and five points respectively. Part of the reason for this lack of trust at work is a lack of belief in the system. Employees report that their demanding work is not being rewarded.

This disillusion spans all types of workers too, as 48 per cent of earners in the top quartile of income, and 49 of those with a college degree or higher believe the system isn't working.

The 2017 Work and Wellbeing Survey from the American Psychological Association surveyed 1,500 employees about their jobs[128]. One of the biggest takeaways from the research was that a lot of employees didn't trust their management team. A third said that during times of change in their organisation, they believed management had a hidden agenda.

A huge one in five said that they did not trust their employer. However, when an organisation recognised the efforts of its employees, and involved them as much as they could, trust was higher. Nick Court, Founder and CEO of Cloud9 People told me that, "trust needs to be embedded in company culture. If an organisation is ever going to have company values, why not have one that says, 'we provide an environment where it is ok to have a go, ok to make mistakes, ok to try a different way'?". Court adds that we should be going further than just encouraging trust, he says we should "praise freedom to act, and criticise micromanagement styles, and actively tell people they have permission to fail as long as they learn, share that learning, and move on". Empowering and trusting employees has been proven to improve their performance time and time again[129].

Employees believe that one of the biggest things an employer can do to most damage trust in them is to pay top executives hundreds of times more than other workers[130]. When asked what employers could be doing to help employees build more trust in a company, 62 per cent of employees said they should treat their people well. This was the highest change employees of all types reported would improve their trust. Trust forms the foundation of any successful relationship. It's one of the most critical issues in human behaviour, and can heavily influence our actions. Organisational trust has become vital to the success of both employee and employer.

Trust is also about the removal of lying in the workplace. According to absence management company Kronos, as many as 58 per cent of employees have called in sick to work just to watch a sporting event[131]. Imagine a workplace that, when an employee didn't want to come to work, an open conversation was had about when that work could be completed and what the trade-off could be. For example, go and watch the football and come in an hour early each day next week to catch up. With more employees than ever working remotely, to do this successfully requires trust. Thirty per cent of employees work away from the office at least a few times a week at present[132], and a manager's requirement to trust their employees is becoming increasingly important. Giving employees the autonomy to do the job as they see fit can really help them. In a Taiwanese study[133], job autonomy has been related to greater work satisfaction, and less intention to leave and seek a job elsewhere.

The empowerment and satisfaction that job autonomy and trust have on an employee can also affect their health. A British study examined the autonomy of employees working at Whitehall in London. Looking at five years' worth of data from more than 7,000 employees, the researchers found that employees who had less control over their job roles showed higher rates of heart disease[134].

Autonomy and trust has become so important to employees that it frequently ranks higher than money and power when someone is looking for a new job. A global study of 2,000 employees found that they were almost two-and-a-half times more likely to take a job that gave them autonomy than a job that gave them influence[135]. In 2017, online employer review site Glassdoor took a sample of more than 600,000 users who submitted an online salary report as well as an employer review. They found that the culture and values of an organisation were the biggest predictors of employee satisfaction. The quality of an organisation's culture and leadership was more important than money[136].

As well as giving employees trust and autonomy, taking it away also has a significant effect. Researchers from the Carleton University in Canada looked at the implications of withdrawing team autonomy in an engineering environment. They found that team autonomy was an 'essential characteristic' of cross-functional teams. Data from 14 different engineering firms showed that the withdrawal of autonomy was negatively correlated with team performance[137].

In their study, Leaders' Perceptions in Organisations in Poland and Russia, Shockley-Zalabak and Morreale concluded that organisations with higher levels of trust are more successful and creative than others[138]. Without trust, an employee's ability to innovate and be entrepreneurial is affected. The atmosphere of distrust created by an organisation can lead to employees bottling things up and not speaking out. This has negative impacts on the sharing of ideas and the psychological safety that we know is so important to employees. Taheri-Lary et al conducted research that indicates there is a meaningful relationship between organisational trust and entrepreneurship[139].

Getting to know our colleagues on a personal level and letting them get to know us is one of the best ways to build a trusting culture in an organisation. So important is it to younger generations, that an organisation's culture should be built on trust and transparency. Trust at work is so important, that on its own it can even influence economic performance[140].

Trust builds compassion, encourages collaboration, improves productivity, and promotes creativity. Trust also promotes more trust. Employees who feel trusted make more effort[141]. The future of any business will rely on its ability to be open and honest with every employee.

10. Fresh Air

USA

For the average American working in a big city like New York, the distance between their home and public transport is a short walk, as is the walk from public transport to the office. For many, that means that they can very easily go an entire day without any real fresh air or interaction with nature. It's commonplace for us to travel while inside a vehicle, work inside, exercise indoors, entertain ourselves indoors and sleep indoors on a day-to-day basis. Statistically, Americans spend 90 per cent of their time indoors[142]. Many of us probably never stop to think about how much time we spend indoors, especially in those countries where the weather usually forces us to stay in. Ninety per cent of our time indoors equates to around 22 hours a day. We'd get almost as much outdoor activity if we were a serious criminal in a US prison.

New research is revealing that the poor, dry indoor air we are breathing so frequently might be causing issues that affect our work. Mental fatigue, tiredness, headaches and sore throats can all be caused by poor air quality. The American Environmental Protection Agency reports that indoor air quality can be as much as five times worse for us than outdoor air[143]. So, despite the pollution we see in so many major cities, that air could still be better for us that staying indoors.

The reason why this air quality can be so poor is that everything we breathe indoors comes mostly from a manmade source. Dust from building materials, carpets, paint, cleaning products, heating and electronic devices all contribute to our poor indoor air quality.

It's been well documented for many years that being outside, and specifically close to nature, has huge benefits for our wellbeing. The Institute for European Environmental Policy, in conjunction with Friends of the Earth Europe, considered the benefits of nature on humans[144]. They compiled all the best research in this field to summarise the surprising health benefits. People living within 300 metres of a green space reported better self-perceived health, and doctors on average prescribe fewer anti-depressants in urban areas with more trees on the street than those without tress. Living close to green areas has seen a reduction in children's behavioural problems, reduction in the development of allergies, lower mental distress and an increase in self-esteem. Unsurprisingly, the research shows that the impact on employees is just as compelling.

For the first time in 2017, a new study revealed just how nature and being outside relaxes our brains[145]. The research looked creating naturalistic conditions including natural sounds etc. They found that these conditions increased parasympathetic activity. The Parasympathetic Nervous System is part of our nervous system that slows down our heart rate, increases glandular and intestinal activity and relaxes some of our muscles.

Ruth Steggles, founder of Fresh Air Fridays told me, "what we see in our work is that when you move employees from the foyer of their office to stand under a tree, their body language changes. Their shoulders drop, and their facial muscles start to relax. We evolved in nature and the artificial lives we now lead, moving quickly between metal and concentre boxes, doesn't serve us. Many people have lost touch with the experience of being outside".

In 2003, the California Energy Commission produced a report that considered office worker performance and the Indoor Environment[146]. The authors found that simply having a view of nature improved an employee's productivity. In call centre environments, they found that those employees who had the best possible view could process 7 to 12 per cent more calls than those without a decent view. They also found that overall, office workers performed 10 to 25 per cent better on tests of mental functioning when they had a pleasant view of nature at work. Aside from the improvement in work performance, those employees with a pleasant view of nature also reported better health and lower fatigue.

A study by the University of Oregon[147] looked at the number of days taken off sick from work, and analysed this data by comparing it to each employee's view from their office. Those employees who had the best natural view from their desks had the least amount of sick days.

The ability to open a window, have a pleasing view, and exposure to natural sun or daylight were all contributing factors. Exposure to sunlight has even also shown to lessen tiredness[148]. Even just the sound of nature can have an enormous impact on us. Research has found that recovery from illness can be faster when exposed to naturally occurring sounds[149].

Dr Joseph Allen at Harvard has studied how indoor air affects people, and he found that the higher the indoor air quality and the better the ventilation, the better decisions people make[150]. In World Green Building Council's Health and Wellbeing and Productivity in Offices report, research from more than 15 different studies have shown a link between improved ventilation and up to 11 per cent improvement in employee productivity. The opposite was also true. Poor ventilation reduced productivity by up to 10 per cent[151]. Humidity too impedes our performance, as it has been seen to reduce our concentration[152].

The charity Mind encourages what it calls 'ecotherapy'. This is an intervention that they say improves the physical health and wellbeing of people by encouraging them to be more active outdoors. In their report Feel Better Outside, Feel Better Inside[153], Mind produces some compelling evidence for providing ecotherapy services to help prevent the development of mental health problems, and to assist with the recovery of existing mental health problems. Ecotherapy has been so effective in some health trusts that the NHS in the UK has implemented a project called 'NHS Forest'.

Funded by charitable trusts, the project aims to improve the health and wellbeing of NHS staff and patients through increasing access to green space on or near NHS-owned land. At the time of writing this book, the charity had planted more than 50,000 trees. With the increasing prevalence of mental health problems among employees, and the impact this is having on employer-sponsored health costs, ecotherapy might be a very cost-effective way for employers to start to manage the issue.

In Japan, there is a growing trend for something the Forestry Ministry called 'Shinrin-Yoku', or 'forest bathing'. Forest bathing is the practice of spending time among nature, specifically trees. People are encouraged to lie on grass under a tree, walk among the cherry blossom, and simply just appreciate all that nature has to offer. So significant has this practice become, that in 1982, it became part of the Japanese Public Health programme. Between 2004 and 2012, the Japanese Government spent around $4 million studying the effects of forest bathing[154]. They measured what are called Human Natural Killer cells (NK) in the immune system. By studying NK before and after exposure to nature and tress, they found some surprising results. Qing Li, a professor at Nippon Medical School in Tokyo found that subjects showed significant increases in NK cell activity after visiting a forest[155]. This is because plants and trees emit phytoncides. These phytoncides are produced to help plants and trees to protect themselves from insects and bacteria, and can improve immune functions in humans.

Research has shown that Shinrin-Yoku can be employed as a stress-reduction method, and even a way of managing depression[156].

There is a hypothesis called 'biophilia' that suggests humans have a built-in desire to want to connect with nature. Popularised by Edward Wilson in 1984, biophilia refers to a love for living things and is becoming a popular tool for workplace design. Incorporating the outside inside when designing workspaces is now so common, the research to back it up is plentiful. Professor Sir Gary Cooper has been studying the impact of biophilic design in the workplace for more than 15 years[157]. Looking at employees from eight EMEA countries, almost half reported having no live plants in the office, and a third no sense of light and space. Those employees who did work in an office with natural elements such as sunlight and plants reported 13 per cent higher wellbeing levels.

The impact nature can have on our overall wellbeing isn't just limited to forests and green spaces. A few years ago, British researchers started to examine how the sea and other 'blue spaces' could improve our lives. Professor Michael Depledge (former Chief Scientist for the Environment Agency), founded the European Centre for Environment and Human Health (ECEHH) in 2011. Soon after, Depledge started the Blue Gym project which looked at the impact water based environments have on people. Initially, Depledge and his team looked at how stress levels were decreased when research participants were shown photographs of green spaces.

He then introduced water to the photographs and found that participants showed a strong preference to the those with more water in them. This initial research was enough to lead to larger studies that show people who live in close proximity to water are healthier than those who don't[158]. It has even been suggested that exposure to any water could be beneficial to our wellbeing, including fountains and water features[159].

Improving natural light and encouraging employees to take breaks away from work to get outside and benefit from fresh, natural air are easy ways to improve the workplace. Another way is to encourage an employee volunteering scheme, as these schemes typically take place outdoors. Employer-backed volunteer schemes enable employees to take paid time off work, get outside and help charitable causes.

Renovating charity buildings, building community gardens, and cleaning up beaches are all popular ways employers can encourage employees to get outside, as well as benefit the community. Volunteering schemes like these can also have other benefits to both employer and employee. A study by Volunteering Australia[160] shows that companies who support employee volunteering find it easier to recruit and retain the best employees. Younger workers are particularly keen to make an impact on society outside of work according to Deloitte[161]. The ONS says that enabling employees to volunteer helps to improve their mental wellbeing by engaging in fulfilling activities[162].

Getting outside in the fresh air and getting closer to nature has clear impacts on every one of us. Despite its obvious risks, the sun also gives huge health benefits to employees who spend adequate time in the sun. The U.S. National Institute of Health recommend about 10 to 15 minutes in the sun. This advice should be taken with the understanding that spending too long in the sun without protection can cause serious health risks. But that's not to say that employees shouldn't make better use of their lunch and coffee breaks to get outside and soak up a small amount of sunshine. Spending tiny amounts of time in the sun will boost an employee's serotonin, the neurotransmitter that regulates sleep, memory and mood. Sunshine also helps us to produce vitamin D which we need to strengthen bones and improve our immune system.

11. Ubuntu

Africa

'Ubuntu' comes from the Nguni Bantu term meaning 'humanity'. Its origins are in the African phrases, 'Motho ke motho ka batho ba bangwe' and 'Umuntu gaunt ngabantu' which mean, 'A person is a person through other persons', or 'I am because we are; we are because I am'[163]. In modern terms, it's used to refer to the idea that people are who they are because of other people and not some higher power. It has also been used to describe the idea of a 'collective responsibility', referring to the idea that we should put the good of our community before ourselves.

Ubuntu is about building relationships that focus on the wellbeing of the whole, whether that is a local community, family or team at work. Head of the South African Truth and Reconciliation Commission, Archbishop Desmond Tutu is credited with bringing this ancient term into the 20th century and into the Western world. Tutu specifically defines Ubuntu as, "affirming of others, not feeling threatened and be assured that you belong as part of the greater whole".

Tutu used the principles of Ubuntu to help bring harmony to Africa, and even Nelson Mandela adopted its principles when he established his new Government in 1994.

In the workplace, the application of Ubuntu can help to tackle the growing HR issue of psychological safety by focusing on the collective efforts of the group through bonding. It does this by promoting the individual's contribution.

It will come to no surprise to any readers that the empirical evidence surrounding teamwork is vast and compelling. As Ubuntu relies on the efforts of a group working as one, it has a part to play in the workplace. Research by the Macrothink Institute[164] in Pakistan reveals a significant positive impact of teamwork on employee performance. Out of four variables (teamwork, spirit de corps, team trust and recognition and reward), teamwork was the most significant independent variable when looking at enhancing employee performance. As usual, what's good for the employee ends up being good for the employer. Collaboration and teamwork produce results and increase productivity. To try and create the perfect team, in 2012 Google embarked on an ambitious project called 'Aristotle'.

Google examined hundreds of their teams to find out the secret to their success. They looked to see if there were any correlations between the best performing teams and factors such as how often they socialised outside of work, what education the team members had and what gender balances existed. Google looked at 180 teams across the world in total, but struggled to find any significant patterns.

It took them a year to find out what they were looking for and they eventually discovered that the most successful teams shared two specific behaviors; team members spoke in the same propositions and team members had “average social sensitivity”. This basically means that everyone had a fair chance to talk and they were all pretty good at working out how other members of the team were feeling. The New York Times reported on Project Aristotle and concluded that if you were faced with two teams (Team A being serious minded and Team B being free flowing) you should opt for Team B, as collectively they will prove to more intelligent than the individual minds of Team A

One of the factors Google discovered in their research has become something that modern businesses are taking very seriously; psychological safety. In a business context, psychological safety is a term that refers to an employee’s comfort when at work. Research shows that the safer an employee feels with other employees, the better they perform. Employees who had psychological safety were more likely to own up to mistakes, less likely to leave, and were more open to ideas. Ubuntu sees a community or group of people as a collective. What Google discovered was that their best performing teams were acting like a singular entity, rather than a collective of people.

Psychological safety is based on the principle that we cannot create a high performing team at work without each member feel safe and feeling part of it. In his book Out of Crisis, author W. Edward Deming created a 14-point management philosophy.

Deming believed that fear in an organisation would hold it back from success and that employers need to encourage openness and honesty. The reluctance to share mistakes, withholding information and blaming others are all recipes for failure. Employers and managers should be nurturing teams that embrace failure and learn from it - as a team.

Research has also started to link psychological safety with social networking theory[165]. Social networking theory is the study of how people interact with each other within their own networks. In the workplace, this could be their team or department. Psychological safety increases with the frequency of communication within a team of employees. Psychological safety also improves the confidence of employees in their own knowledge. Encouraging a culture of psychological safety can motivate employees to share more knowledge with their team members.

There is a saying at the Disney Corporation: "Treat employees like customers". Bruce Jones, Senior Programming Director at the Disney Institute says, "in our experience, the best way for companies to create emotional connections with their customers is by ensuring that every interaction delights them. To do that, you need more than great products – you need motivated, empowered people at the front line"[166]. Disney recognised a long time ago that the only way they could deliver the kind of service required to be 'the happiest place on earth', was if their own employees were happy.

One of the things Disney set out to do was to listen with purpose. It's a Disney manager's job to get personally involved in tackling their employees' issues and needs.

Being able to develop an interpersonal relationship with their employees (like they do at Disney) requires managers to have elevated levels of emotional intelligence – a skill that is fast becoming very desirable. Emotional intelligence is our capacity to be aware of, and handle other people's emotions with empathy.

In Google's internal research into what makes a good manager, they identified that listening to teams, helping employees and expressing an interest in their wellbeing, as some of the core skills that led to success[167]. Leadership that has a basis in emotional intelligence can have an enormous impact on an organisation's culture. Managers who have high emotional intelligence communicate more effectively and make better decisions[168].

As early as the late 1990s, psychologists started exploring the benefits of psychological safety, particularly when related to teamwork. In 1999, Harvard psychologist Amy Edmondson[169] first coined the term after she examined 51 teams in a manufacturing company. Edmondson discovered that learning behaviour mediates between team psychological safety and team performance. Interpersonal trust and mutual respect characterises the right kind of climate for employees to bloom. The key to building teams where psychological safety is common is to start by being inclusive.

Making sure everyone has a say and is involved in decision making rank among the most crucial factors. Therefore, it is no surprise that Ubuntu has survived so many centuries in Africa. The only surprise is why it took the rest of us so long to catch on.

12. Happiness

Bhutan

One of the most well-known documents created by man is the United States Declaration of Independence. I've been lucky enough to see it in person in Washington D.C, and to this day one line still resonates with me; "life, liberty and the pursuit of Happiness". For many Americans, it is poignant because it reminds us all that we strive every day to be happy. However, some experts have suggested that the 'happiness' the document refers to, might not be what we initially thought. It is suggested that in 1776 (when the declaration was written) the common meaning of 'happiness' was possibly to mean 'prosperity, thriving and wellbeing'[170]. In the 21st Century, happiness is linked more with material gains and status, than it is our wellbeing.

Patrick Phelan, Co-Founder at The Happiness Index says, "happiness means something different to everyone and so it's a matter of perspective". To be able to measure happiness, we really need to understand what is actually is.

In Bhutan, the Government believes happiness refers to much more than just a way we feel. They feel happiness is so important that they now measure countrywide prosperity by gauging happiness.

The Government of Bhutan looked at gross national happiness (GNH) and the spiritual, physical, social and environmental health of its people as a measure of progress. Since 1971, this Buddhist country has been focused on the wellbeing of its people over material growth.

Bhutan's ideas started to gain worldwide attention in 2011 when the United Nations showed interest in its ideas, as Bhutan had achieved noteworthy results in its aim to extend life expectancy. Bhutan came up with the idea of a GNH index and its nine domains:

1. Psychological Wellbeing
2. Health
3. Education
4. Time Use
5. Cultural Diversity and Resilience
6. Good Governance
7. Community Validity
8. Ecological Diversity and Resilience
9. Living Standards

By measuring people into four groups - unhappy, narrowly happy, extensively happy and deeply happy, the index explores how policy changes can increase happiness across the nation.

For employees and employers alike, looking at the above domains will immediately reveal some similarities between them and the most progressive HR and engagement strategies. Looking after the happiness and overall wellbeing of employees has long been a focus of organisations hoping to get the most of their employees.

Even Google have Chief Happiness Officers to ensure their employees' wellbeing and happiness is catered for, and others are following suit. Block Chain have recently appointed a Director of Happiness to retain the 'specialness' of Millennials in particular[171]. Phelan says "employees will never be able to be fully effective for an organisation if they are not happy. However, they also need to be engaged at work. If your employees are happy and engaged, then you will have a productive employee and a productive organisation". It stands to reason that a happy employee is a better employee and that promoting happiness at work would produce a more productive workforce.

Employers need to be taking some responsibility for their employees' happiness, because happiness matters for employees, customers and the bottom line according to Nick Gianoulis, Founder and 'Godfather of Fun' at The Fun Dept. and co-author of Playing It Forward. Gianoulis says, "leadership buy-in is the first law of fun and happiness at work. Where leaders are bought in, we have experienced a 100 per cent success rate in improving engagement, retention and other desirable business outcomes".

Gianoulis says a happy employee is 44 per cent more likely to stay with an employer than those that are not. He adds, "a whopping 81 per cent of employees in companies rated 'great' in Fortunes Best 100 Places to Work For, reported working in a 'fun' environment". Having fun at work makes us work harder.

According to the University of Warwick[172], there is a good reason behind why we work harder when we are happy. In the first experiment of its kind, researchers spent time with random participants and made them happier. Some were shown a 10-minute film based on the routines of a well-known British comedian and others were given treats like chocolate to eat. The other groups were asked to talk about sad moments in their lives like the death of a loved one to reduce their happiness levels. Researchers then measured how productive these random participants were after by asking them to add a series of five two-digit numbers together in an allotted time. Their fee for participating was based on the number of correct answers they submitted. They found that those participants who were 'happy' had 12 per cent more productivity than those who weren't. The 'unhappy' participants showed productivity levels of 10 per cent lower than the placebo group. The researchers concluded that lower happiness is systematically associated with lower productivity.

Peter Jenkinson, Business Development Director, Wrkit, thinks a lack of employee happiness causes presenteeism.

"Presenteeism is the malaise of the modern workforce, damaging company performance, negatively effecting company culture, and causing workplace stress". Presenteeism refers to employees who come to work, but malinger or don't actually do much work at all. It's typically associated with employees who are disengaged or simply just don't want to be at work. These are typically unhappy employees.

Why happiness makes people more productive is an area of much debate, but many psychologists agree that unhappiness (at least) leads to a lack of concentration. They believe the idea of worry is linked with distraction. Talking to The Guardian newspaper, lead researcher for the study Andrew Oswald said, "positive emotions appear to invigorate human beings, while negative emotions have the opposite effect"[173]. Positivity at work makes employees happier.

Since this first study in happiness and productivity was published, organisations around the world have reported comparable results. This can be seen quite clearly when looking at Forbes 100 Best Companies to work for. Those companies that feature in the list have seen 14 per cent year on year stock price increases compared to just six percent for the market overall. Jenkinson told me that ensuring employees are happy is quite simple: "Culture, culture, culture! Forbes tell us that there are seven ways to ensure employees are happy[174]. I disagree, there is one way; foster and observe a culture that encourages diversity, engagement, reward, development and fun!"

The research into disengagement at work isn't to be taken lightly. For over 30 years and with 30 million employees taking part, Gallup[175] have produced one of the most significant and long-term studies into employee happiness, engagement and wellbeing we have ever seen. As a result, Gallup have produced some eye-opening statistics that employers should be paying attention to. Gallup estimates that disengaged employees are costing American businesses more than $300 billion in lost productivity every year.

In the United States, the Gallup-Heathways Well-being Index has been polling more than 1,000 adults every day since 2008. Overall, in 2016, wellbeing in the US hit a record high as the index showed fewer smokers than ever before and an increase in people's rates of exercise. However, chronic diseases like depression were at their highest ever rates since the index began. Despite improvements in their physical health, Americans are starting to suffer from other health complexities related to the stresses of everyday life and the pressures of work.

One of the biggest studies of its kind has just been completed to consider what makes for a happy and healthy life. The Harvard Study of Adult Development tracked the lives of 724 men for 78 years – one of the longest psychological studies ever conducted[176]. As well as conducting regular medicals, scans and blood tests, the researchers also interviewed the men every few years on their mental and physical health, their jobs, friendships and relationships.

The study's Director Robert J. Waldinger has shared what he thinks the secrets to a happy life are:

A happy childhood

The impact of a happy childhood had positive effects well into adult life. Having a close relationship with parents during childhood often leads to closer relationships as we grow older.

This can also be true if we have close relationships with at least one sibling, and both are predictors of happiness in later life. Interestingly, even those people who don't have happy childhoods, can positively impact their own future later in life.

The researchers found that those men brought up in poverty or with chaotic families had the opportunity to engage in what they called 'generativity' – an interest in building a connection with, and guiding, younger generations. Those men that reached 50-plus who did this reported to be happier and more well-adjusted.

Developing stress management techniques

Coping with stress is something we all must try and master at some point in our lives. However, the researchers in this study found that there were a few ways of coping with stress that impacted happiness more than others. They called these adaptive methods and list them as:

Sublimation – An example might be where an employee feels unfairly treated at work, so they start an organisation that helps protect workers' rights.

Altruism – An example might be an alcoholic staying sober by being a sponsor for another.

Suppression – A example might be in an organisation that is making job cuts, an employee puts these worries out of their mind until they can do something about them.

Those men who used these methods reported having better relationships with others; it made them easier to be with and led to more social support. It also helped make older men healthier in later life, and kept their brains sharper for longer.

According to Waldinger, the single most significant predictor of a happy life was the quality and quantity of a person's relationships. Time spent with others was considered by the participants as being the most meaningful part of their lives. Spending time with other people on a day to day basis buffers us against the mood dips that come with everyday life, and even the physical pain of getting older. Our relationships with a partner or spouse are of importance. Employers can learn a great deal from this study and develop ways of ensuring they are doing what they can to encourage an employee's happiness. For the first time ever, we have five generations of workers in the workplace.

There are numerous benefits to having a varied workforce, but now we can see that encouraging older people to mentor and work alongside your younger employees can aid their wellbeing and happiness.

We couldn't have a chapter on happiness without talking about money. Oprah.com has described the pressure young people face over money as "the new midlife crisis"[177]. More than any other age group, Generation X (those born between 1965 and 1984) carry more debt[178]. I interviewed ITV's money expert and Founder and CEO of financial wellbeing service Moola, Gemma Godfrey, about why we perceive money to be so closely linked to happiness.

Godfrey says, "healthy finances are essential for a happy, healthy life. This is because money is needed to satisfy our fundamental needs. We want to feel secure and free to do what is needed to look after ourselves". Godfrey adds, "money underlies most major decisions we make in life – where we can live, how much we can provide for our family and the lifestyle we can lead". Godfrey believes that money can shape how we feel and how we act. The interesting thing about money and happiness is that the two are related, but not in the way you might expect.

For centuries, society has linked money with happiness. However, a recent study by Princeton University revealed that our happiness related to income stops and levels out at $75,000[179].

Analysis of 450,000 Americans found that most of them (85 per cent) felt happy daily, regardless of their income. However, they also found that although earning less money didn't directly cause unhappiness, it did make the participants feel generally more ground down by the burdens of everyday life. It was only when a participant was earning $75,000 that those feelings started to disappear. More recently this figure has been increased to $83,000[180], but the sentiment remains the same; if employees are earning a decent wage, this can contribute (in part) to their happiness.

In 2015, CEO of credit card processing company, Gravity Payments made the bold step of responding to the research mentioned above and decided to give all his employees a minimum of $70,000 a year. Dan Price made headlines around the world, and inevitably picked up a lot of new clients. However, for Price, this move was more about making his employees feel safe and happy than it was about PR. Two and a half years after making the move, Price explained the effect it had on him, his business and his employees in a LinkedIn post[181]. Price said, "employees whose salaries rose under the new policy, have experienced a noticeable improvement in their quality of life and have been able to do the things they'd previously had to put off for financial reasons".

Price saw that more younger employees were starting families than ever before in the company, and more Millennials were buying their first homes. He was changing lives one by one. They even saw his employees' 401(k) contributions increase significantly.

Price says, "it's evident that, by reducing the anxiety inherent in laying a retirement nest egg, our team can now turn their attention toward more fulfilling activities". I don't think Price's decision was about paying people more money, this was about removing worry and stress caused by the differences in salaries and the inflated cost of living. All Price did was remove that burden and the price he had to pay to do it was $70k per employee.

However, it's not only the amount of money that a person has, but how they manage it that leads to increased happiness. Jo Thresher, Director of Better with Money says, "problem debt affects every part of our life and will of course affect an employee's ability to work productively, to be engaged, and it can even affect their safety at work". Thresher adds, "if we have money concerns, it pervades everything we do". Helping employees manage their money better can lead to happiness. Good money management can free up funds to enable employees to pay for someone else to do some of their chores – a happiness that research says money can buy. Research published in the Proceedings of the National Academy of Science of the United States of America in 2017[182] found that relieving the time pressure modern employees feel is the key to their happiness.

According to research, employers can invest in and encourage employees to spend money on things that save them time like a cleaner and eating out. These things have been shown to help to ease the burden of modern day stress and improve happiness[183].

The key to removing unhappiness caused by money is also to encourage higher financial literacy. Higher financial literacy has been shown to lead to increased financial wellbeing and fewer financial concerns[184]. Having fewer financial concerns is important because most people often rate their financial situation as their biggest cause of unhappiness.

We've discussed employees' sleep patterns quite a bit in this book as it's clear that the only way an employee can remain present and productive at work is after a period of quality rest. But it also might be the secret ingredient to our happiness too. The National Centre for Social Research surveyed thousands of UK residents to see what contributed to 'living well'[185]. They found that the average Brit has a 'living well score' of around 62 out of 100, with the highest 20 per cent of people scoring between 72 and 92.

As we've seen, having more money shouldn't have an impact on someone's happiness, and the results of this study show the same. A person's income has a trivial effect on their living well score. However, improved sleep quality led to a living well score equivalent to having four times as much disposable income. This is important because according to a poll published in The Guardian newspaper, money is the UK's biggest worry[186]. For the younger generations, it's a big source of unhappiness. More than half of all Millennials worry about money 'most of the time' and are having sleepless nights because of it[187].

Research even suggests that the worry caused by money is so prevalent that it's the leading cause of stress among American workers, regardless of how much they earn[188]. Worrying about money is causing employees to be unhappy and it's affecting their work. Global bank Barclays looked at the impact these financial concerns are having on employees' abilities to do their job. They found that one in 10 employees are struggling financially and two in 10 believe this is affecting their work[189].

Godfrey believes that employers should be taking some of the responsibility for ensuring their employees' financial wellbeing is improving, and this starts with helping them make the most of what money they have. "The good news is the guidance on how to do this, and the tools for action have never been easier to access. Modern technology means there are online services (like Moola!), that offer saving and investing tips for free, as well as the ability to set aside as little as £50 and give it a chance to grow in value. The earlier employees get started, the more manageable the amount they need to save to achieve their money goals".

Over the past few years, I've dedicated a generous portion of my working life to assisting employers with their financial wellbeing strategy. It's clear that if we are to encourage employees to be happy, we need to consider what is making them unhappy, and for many, money is one of an employee's biggest concerns. Despite the improvements of the economy after the economic downturn, Brexit has made consumers and the economy unstable again.

This has led employees to have new concerns about their financial future. Godfrey believes employers should be helping their employees because, "preparing for the future brings peace of mind and offers employees the freedom to live the life they choose.". An employee's financial wellbeing is ever changing as the demands of life come and go. Employers can help employees prepare for this uncertain future.

The important thing for employers to realise is that the best financial wellbeing strategies are designed to help employees take responsibility for, and prepare for the future. Godfrey says, "whether it's affording that home deposit, a child's education or just sleeping well at night knowing they're making smarter decisions with their money. Getting better informed and taking back control by doing something about it can make all the difference to employee wellbeing".

To remove the stress or worry from an employee's life or just taking steps to help them improve their happiness, employers need to find out what makes their employees happy or unhappy. As we've already learned in this chapter, giving employees frequent opportunities to spend time together as humans and not just colleagues can help to create meaningful experiences, relationships and a support network. This socialising and support can also help to create stress coping mechanisms as employees seek to support each other through challenging times - especially when the worry relates to finances[190]. Happy people make for productive and innovative employees.

A person's personality can frequently be found in their work, so ensuring employees are happy and free from financial stress means they can deliver the best service to their customers.

13. Employee Benefits

UK

Having dedicated a sizable portion of my career to enhancing the employee benefit provision, I couldn't leave it out of this book. With some of the most advanced company-provided benefits packages in the world, the UK teaches us our next lesson, and it started in the 19th century. Over 100 years ago, a movement was started by small groups of philanthropists that would lead to such huge changes in the workplace that employees across the world still benefit from them today. Some of these changes have been lost over time, and it seems that some of the new, popular trends in improving the workplace aren't that new at all. Our renewed focus on employee wellbeing for example, is something we started, forgot about, and revived recently.

Welsh social reformer Robert Owen became one of the founders of the UK cooperative movement, and as it seems, a forerunner of employee experience and engagement. Owen first worked in the cotton industry in Manchester and in his twenties married the daughter of the proprietor of a large mill at New Lanark, Scotland. He worked his way up to management level and started playing a big part in the Mill's day to day operations. When Owen eventually took over the business, the general condition of its employees was poor.
The plans Owen had for improving the lives of his employees displeased his business partners because they were expensive.

Nevertheless, Owen started to seek to improve conditions for his employees through workplace benefits. Owen was aware that happy employees were more committed, productive and more engaged at work. Owen was fighting bitter objections from all over the country. At the time, the well-known economist Nassau Senior said that increased costs at the mills would ruin the industry, which made a major contribution to the wealth of the country. This was later found to be wrong, as better fed, less tired workers produced more, not less.

New working regulations were drafted by Owen, raising the age of employment to 10 years old, limiting the working day to 10 hours and introducing factory inspections. Owen's methods were revolutionary and soon caught the attention of Sir Robert Peel. It was Peel who persuaded Parliament to set up a committee to enquire into factory conditions, and Robert Owen and many other mill owners like him were asked to give evidence. This resulted in the Factories Act in 1819 and inspections to ensure the regulations were being adhered to. This was one of the most significant changes to working life the UK had ever seen. The idea of offering benefits to a workforce for the advantage of both employee and employer was founded. So far ahead of his time was he, Owen even realised the impact he could have in the workplace by improving the lives of his employees outside of work.

Over the last five years in the UK, focus on employee financial wellbeing has become a big trend because of its roots in employee stress and unhappiness. As we learned in the last chapter, financial concerns are frequently topping the list of things that keep employees awake at night.

Owen realised the importance of investing in improving the financial wellbeing of his employees. Owen even funded social activities outside work, because he knew how important it was to have happy, stress-free workers. Unlike other mills at the time, Owen paid his staff in money rather than tokens, so they could spend it wherever they liked, not just mill-owned businesses. Owen also set up local shops for employees where prices were 25 per cent lower than elsewhere to enable employees' pay to go further. Ensuring his employees didn't worry about life was a priority for Owen. The removal of worry plays an important part in the happiness of employees.

Owen ploughed his profits back into his schemes to fund education and only sold local produce to pay back to the community. Owen was the first major employer to offer:

- Free healthcare for employees
- Onsite crèche for working mothers
- Evening classes for adult workers
- Social events for staff

In 1816, Owen opened the first infant school in Great Britain at the New Lanark Mills and gave it his close personal supervision. Owen believed that if the parents were happy and not worrying about childcare, they would pay more attention at work. The schools, which did away with corporal punishment, emphasised character development and included dancing and music in their curriculum. Workplace nurseries are now commonplace in the UK and act as a great attraction and retention tool for new parents.

On his deathbed, Owen was asked by a Minister if he regretted wasting his life on 'fruitless projects'. At the time, many saw his ideas as too socialist and he wasn't a popular man. Owen responded to the Minister saying, "my life was not useless; I gave important truths to the world, and it was only for want of understanding that they were disregarded. I have been ahead of my time". Ahead of his time he was. Owen gained international recognition for his work in improving conditions for UK employees and his schemes led to a worldwide attitude change as well as legal reform that we still see today.

More than 100 years after Owen's first venture into improving the employee experience, millions of hours of research have been dedicated to how better working conditions can make employees happier and more productive. One of the most significant working practices Owen changed that we still stick by today is the length of our working day.

In 1817, Owen had created the eight-hour day, and coined the slogan, “eight hours’ labour, Eight hours’ recreation, Eight hours’ rest”. Soon after, Henry Ford picked up on the idea and the eight-hour work day was formalised around the world.

The provision of employee benefits continues to be one of the most significant investments employers make in their employees. Peter Jenkinson, Business Development Director, Wrkit says, “choosing employee benefits and creating easy access to these benefits has an enormous and disproportionally positive effect on presenteeism, performance and employee Net Promoter Score (eNPS)”. For many multinational organisations, benefits spend tops more than $10 million[191]. Even smaller employers are investing in employee benefits. Towry Law report that UK small to medium companies spend almost £1 billion annually on employee benefits[192]. Investment in employee benefits is an investment in attracting and retaining employees.

According to MetLife, 83 per cent of employers say retaining employees is their top objective by offering benefits[193] and it seems to be working. Willis Towers Watson report that 75 per cent of employees say they’re more likely to stay with their employer because of their benefit programme[194]. Reward Consultant and Founder at Road to Green, Scott Baker says, “over the last decade, employee benefits have grown in importance to attract and retain talent.

For the modern reward team, it is essential to be aware of trends in the employee benefits market whilst exploring and understanding the needs of their own employee population. The challenge is to offer flexibility and choice within a considered benefits framework that is both competitive versus the market, and appropriate for the organisation. Communicating clearly, linking to company identity and culture is crucial to achieve maximum engagement and take-up, and to deliver value for money to the organisation".

The 2017 Employee Benefits Magazine research revealed that a massive 82 per cent of employers believe employee benefits are an effective retention tool[195]. Employees feel the same too - especially where benefits are related to health. Just 11 per cent of US employees don't have health insurance[196]. Because of the cost of health insurance in America, this benefit has become a vital requirement for employees and they are attracted to employers who offer this benefit specifically. Eighty-seven per cent of American workers report that employment based health insurance is extremely or very important to them[197]. However, as the workplace changes and more and more younger employees enter the workforce, the desire for these types of benefits are decreasing. The Employee Benefit Research Institute reports that younger workers are more likely to choose benefits like paid time off[198]. Sixty-four per cent of young workers say benefits are extremely or very important to employer loyalty[199].

Kathryn Kendall, Chief People Officer at Benefex told me, "I think what a lot of employers fail to realise is just how much a well-chosen set of employee benefits can personalise the reward package for their employees". Kendall believes the personalisation of employee benefits is a component of a great employee experience. Kendall adds, "when it comes to reward, it can be a real challenge to stand out from our competitors. Base salary, car allowance, bonus scheme and pension. These form our hygiene factors – they're the minimum that an employee expects – but what they don't do is mark us as an employer of choice or differentiate our employee brand. That's where our wider employee benefits package comes in".

The provision of employee benefits has become a vital component of employment for many workers. In the UK, as pressure on the National Health Service and the state grows, employees are being encouraged to find their own healthcare and retirement provision. The expectation that the Government will support a sick worker is false, and this is leading to an increase in the number of employer sponsored critical illness and income protection schemes.

With around one in 10 new cancer cases being among adults aged 25 to 49 years old[200], the protection of our lives and our health is no longer something that is of interest to just the older employees. Offering employee benefits that don't just support but protect the wellbeing of employees is now commonplace.

Employee benefits are also no longer the provision of large corporates, as more than 99 per cent of all UK businesses are now a small to medium business (SME). There is growing adoption of benefits to employees of these smaller organisations. On the back of pensions auto enrolment in the UK, there is a growing trend for SMEs to offer more complex benefits packages aimed at improving the overall health and wellbeing of their staff.

ResearchMoz say that, "uncertainty among employees working in SMEs, attributed to negligible monthly savings they make, is a key factor stoking the demand for employee benefits in the UK"[201]. In early 2017, I spoke to Professional Pensions about this growing trend[202]. I told the magazine that I think there has been an increase in demand for employee benefits within SMEs because we have more SMEs in the country. Innovative technology startups are dominating the workplace and need to work hard to tempt talent away from large corporates. Offering a decent benefits scheme is an effective way to do this.

In 2017, it's hard to imagine a world where employers didn't seek to improve the lives of their employees. Offering a good employee benefits scheme has advantages to employees inside and outside of work, from reducing the cost of everyday living to easing the stress of work. Employees who are very satisfied with their employee benefits are four times more likely to be satisfied with their jobs[203].

The demands of an increasingly diverse workforce are traditionally met through an employer's benefits scheme. Regardless of age or income, employees can secure their financial future, protect their retirement or insure their families against the worst through employee benefits.

14. Lie In

Australia

We've looked at the potential benefits of a shorter working day, but are there benefits to both employer and employee by just starting the day a bit later? In 2016, DEPUTY conducted a study that looked at 400,000 different workers to understand how many Australians were late for work[204]. They discovered that a huge 40 per cent of them started work later than they were supposed to. DEPUTY reported that this volume of lateness could represent significant productivity losses for Australian businesses. With more than half of employees blaming traffic and simply not being able to get out of bed in time as the reason behind their lateness, could encouraging employees to just start the working day later be a solution? It certainly could be when we consider that the eight-hour working day no longer appears to be working. According to news.com.au, the average Australian is spending less time at work than they were 10 years ago, but are working more hours[205].

In Australia, schools have been trialing later starting times to allow students to make the most of their learning. Education Minister Martin Dixon has shown his support for more flexible days for students. The Sun Herald newspaper[206] reported in 2014 that several Australian schools were starting to adopt later or staggered starting times.

This trend to allow students to start school later has been catching on for a while around the world.

In the US, more than 80 districts have introduced later high school start times since the turn of the century. In the Journal of Developmental & Behavioral Pediatrics[207], researchers showed that a 25-minute delay in school start times resulted in significantly reduced sleepiness among students, and improved sleep and daytime functioning in teenagers. The trend to accommodate later start times has now flowed into assessing the working day for adults as these teenagers move into the workforce. The research into allowing employees to start work later than the traditional 9am is very compelling as, "work is the number one sleep killer", says Dr Mathias Basner, an assistant professor of sleep and chronobiology in psychiatry at the University of Pennsylvania Perelman School of Medicine. In his research[208], Basner surveyed 125,000 American employees and discovered that work is the main activity they exchanged for sleep.

In September 2015, Dr Paul Kelley from Oxford University gave a speech at the British science festival. Kelley suggests we all have what he calls a natural Circadian rhythm. Kelley says this is an internal body clock that regulates our behaviour, including patterns of eating, sleeping, and waking. By adjusting our working day to start at a time which fits in with our Circadian rhythm, Kelley says we could see an improvement in cognitive performance.

Kelley says, "we cannot change our 24-hour rhythms. You cannot learn to get up at a certain time. Your body will be attuned to sunlight and you're not conscious of it because it reports to hypothalamus, not sight". Kelley's research suggests that any employee under the age of 55 should be aiming to start work at 10am to make the most out of the working day[209]. In the UK and the US, one in three employees suffers from poor sleep[210], so an extra few hours' sleep might make all the difference.

A study by RAND Europe[211] has reinforced the idea that lack of sleep impairs an employee's productivity, and can even inhibit the economy. The study examined figures from the UK, US, Canada, Germany and Japan, and looked to try and quantify the economic loss due to lack of employee sleep. The results were eye-opening. In the US alone, it's estimated that one million work days a year are lost to due to inadequate sleep. That equates to a huge $11 billion per year. As we learned at the start of this book, the worldwide economy is already suffering from a lack of productivity, so any ideas to fill this gap should be carefully considered.

Most recently, the Academy of Management Review published a new study that introduced the world to the concept of 'Chronotype Diversity'[212]. This concept states that people are biologically predisposed to work better at varying times of the day. The researchers in this study looked at how a team's performance can be affected by each team member's biological predisposition to working or resting at various parts of the day.

The researchers set out to prove that this diversity of chronotypes could have a positive or negative impact on overall team performance. Recognising this difference in team members' chronotype diversity could be the key to unlocking the secret to enhanced performance in employees.

Organisations could start by identifying which team members like to start early or finish earlier, and structure the team and its work accordingly. In an interview about the body's circadian rhythm, Dr Stefan Volk from the University of Sydney told The Huffington Post, "this biological pattern also determines when we are highly attentive and have our mental performance peaks, and when we are exhausted and tired"[213].

In an anecdote published by Thrive Global[214], Founding Partner and CEO and ICONIQ Capital, Michael Anders, spoke about a pact he made with his children. In 2016, Anders agreed to walk his children to school every single day. After the first time he did this, he said something had changed for him. He reported having "a sense of purpose beyond the usual". It wasn't long before this morning task became the most important of his day and took priority over everything else. By allowing himself to start work later to accommodate this change, Anders not only positively impacted the daily lives of his children, but he gained enormous satisfaction from it. He said this change didn't come at the expense of his business, but made him more productive and efficient at work.

Nick Court, Founder and CEO of Cloud9 People says, "remember, discretional effort does not necessarily mean extra hours. Let people know it's ok to start later or leave earlier, and ask that all people (including the leaders) do this and do this visibly. Start with a 'yes' when people ask to start work later, and remember that what is important to you may be different to what other people value". As we learned from the Japanese, a sense of purpose and a reason to get up and go to work is one of the strongest features of a great employee experience.

As I researched for this book, I found many recent studies that show how loss of sleep has a surprising impact of our ability to function normally. Even just losing one and a half hours of the sleep that our body needs each night drops our daytime alertness by one third. Giving employees the opportunity to sleep more, and have better quality sleep can help to tackle the huge productivity problem that most of the world is currently facing. This is especially important when we consider that most employees leave jobs for preventable reasons like not having a decent work-life balance[215]. Employees are even willing to take less money in return for an improved work-life balance - $7,600 a year to be exact[216].

Accommodating the biological differences of a diverse workforce, or simply just the preferences of team members, might be an effortless way to ensure that all team members are functioning to the best of their ability.

As flexible working becomes one of the most requested benefits of employment, it's easy to see how an employer who offers the chance to work in tandem with your own Circadian rhythm could have a huge competitive advantage. Scott Baker, Reward Consultant and Founder at Road to Green agrees; "For me this [flexible working] is essential. When I have managed teams in the past, other than routine weekly catch-ups I prefer to allow my team to fully manage their time and workload.

This may vary depending on individual experience and how much guidance is required, but I believe that empowerment and freedom within the workplace allow for greater development opportunities, and ultimately bring out the best in people". In the future world of work, where more and more employees are adopting remote working, this might be an ideal way to accommodate these circadian differences.

Flexible working is currently soaring in popularity, and this has prompted a new wave of research dedicated to extolling its virtues. A recent study by Cardiff University showed that almost three quarters of employees say they put more effort in when working from home[217]. The study examined 15,000 responses from employees from 2001, 2006 and 2012, and concluded that those employees working from home put in extra effort and worked longer hours. Despite the extra hours, employees also reported that they were happier with these types of arrangements.

I discussed flexible working and the future of work with Jacob Morgan as part of his global 'The Future If' online group[218]. Morgan said, "employees want flexible work. It's especially important to millennials and younger workers. They love the idea of being able to work without being chained to a desk or a 9-5 schedule. As Director, Global Partnerships at Benefex Gethin Nadin points out, with every other aspect of work changing over the last 100 years, it's crazy that the standard work schedule hasn't been updated with the times. Companies with flexible work programs are able to attract and retain top employees and keep morale and productivity high. Employees tend to stay longer at companies with these types of programs and actually get their work done.".

However, despite its growing popularity, employees in the UK in particular are finding it difficult to arrange flexible working. The TUC reports that young parents are turning to flexible working as they are finding it hard to arrange childcare around core working hours[219]. However, the report revealed that two out of five respondents who had asked their employer for flexible working, felt they were penalised as a result. We still have a long way to go if we are to try and change our century long attitude to the working day.

The ability to stop and start our working day at a time that works best for the employee clearly has benefits. In the UK, telecoms giant BT has offered its staff flexible working for several years. BT now has around seven out of 10 employees working flexibly – that's about 70,000 people.

In their flexible working report[220], BT Chairman Sir Christopher Bland says, "it [flexible working] has saved the company millions in terms of increased productivity and cut costs. It has also motivated our people and released more potential".

It seems the Australians really are onto something when they let their employees have that extra few hours in bed.

15. Technology

USA

Technology is now entwined in our working lives. For a large portion of the workforce (those employees born after 1980 in particular), technology has played a big part of their lives from birth. These employees are referred to as 'digital natives'. Sixty-eight per cent of Americans now have smartphones and 45 per cent have tablet computers[221]. However, with more and more bits of technology being added to the workplace as well as at home, employees are starting to suffer with technology overload. According to the latest research, we now spend almost half our waking hours using technology. The average time awake for an adult is around 15 hours and 45 minutes, and we spend an amazing 45 per cent of that time using technology[222].

While conducting research for his book, Jacob Morgan identified workplace technology as one of the three principal areas of the employee experience. Employees deserve the same digital experience they get as consumers, in the workplace. However, many employers are still failing to invest in technology to improve the lives of their employees. Kathryn Kendall, Chief People Officer at Benefex says, "I think we have a real issue with technology in that we tend to polarise our opinions.

Technology is either the hero of the piece and the catch all solution to all our problems, or it is demonised and blamed for everything which is wrong in society. The reality is somewhere in between. Technology can be a hugely powerful tool for us as we start to create the workplaces of tomorrow, but it has to be used with caution".

Technology has become so important to our working lives, that our reliance on it can be the source of great advantage but also great discontent. Research shows that if the technology we use at work is old or not fit for purpose, it can demoralise employees. That is why it's become so central to the employee experience. When technology becomes hard to use, it causes employees to become frustrated, which research says can affect productivity, employee mood, and even their interactions with their co-workers[223].

Ensuring the technology employees use at work is up-to-date and of a high standard has become vital. A growing trend in HR is called the 'New Work Concept'. This is based around the idea that employees are increasingly more efficient and productive when they are connected by technology. This makes those employees who are familiar with technology a more attractive hiring prospect. The new pace of work and expectation from employees requires HR to keep up with technological advancements. This technology must be up-to-date, work with the most advanced devices, and importantly provide a good, quick user experience. According to the New York Times, people will visit a website less often if it is slower than a competitor's by more than just 250 milliseconds[224].

It is clear that our familiarity with technology has led us to have little-to-no patience for old or outdated tech.

In 2016, researchers reported that British people were losing their patience with slow and outdated technology more than ever. It takes just 60 seconds for the average person to lose their temper when technology doesn't respond the way they expect it to[225]. When workplace technology becomes hard to use, it causes employees frustration, negatively impacts productivity and affects an employee's mood[226]. The prevalence of workplace technology means this frustration is likely already being felt by our employees.

It's estimated that more than 40 per cent of an employee's time spent using technology at work is wasted due to a poor user experience. With the average organisation using around 508 different cloud technologies[227], that's a lot that is wasted. As cloud technology has boomed in popularity, organisations are struggling to manage so many different platforms and vendors. There is a growing trend for organisations to deliver more in one place, with PwC reporting that 40 per cent of employers in 2017 are seeking to reduce the number of cloud technology vendors they use[228]. Consolidation of these systems can make an enormous difference to the employee experience. According to The State of Workplace Productivity Report[229] published by Cornerstone OnDemand, 38 per cent of employees say there isn't enough technology collaboration in the workplace.

Employees' access to affordable, market-leading technology and fast internet access at home, has led to a desire to have the same in the workplace. According to Salesforce's State of the Connect Customer report, more than 70 per cent of employees say they want the same technology in the workplace that they use at home[230]. The fast adoption of technology in our home lives is leading to huge changes at work. Cloud and internet technology has taken over human resources, and it's making us better at our jobs. Forty-six per cent of employed adults in the USA say the internet has made them more productive at work[231].

From my experience, I estimate that employees typically access as many as 15 different technologies just to be able to manage standard HR transactions like booking a vacation or checking a payslip. Kendall told me, "what technology has started to do is to free up the time of HR teams, allowing them to move away from manual processing and instead focus their attentions on delivering a stand out employee experience" Kendall believes technology is going to transform the way we work. "We need to embrace the future of technology without losing the authenticity of a personal interaction". Kendall added, "when we can utilise technology to deliver a seamless process for our employees, which gives them what they need, when they need it – *and* still keep the human touch – that's when we really start to drive value, for both employees and employer".

By consolidating all HR technologies into one single platform, employees can remove the frustration associated with remembering multiple URLs and passwords. In addition, the user experience of some platforms is so outdated and difficult to navigate that employees just don't use them.

Consumers in the UK and USA have seen the collaboration trend as organisations like Google start to encourage users to email, save documents, and share content etc. all in one place. Having worked in the HR technology space for most of my working life, I've seen the impact technology has had on improving the lives of employees and employers.

Technology has reduced time spent on HR administration by up to 50 per cent, and reduced administrative costs by around 40 per cent[232]. This increase in efficiency has resulted in large cost savings and easier access to data. This has meant that (possibly for the first time), HR managers are able to mine data and make much more informed policy decisions in real time. Understanding trends in data from things like why employees are leaving and who needs training has led to improvements in the workplace. As the recruitment and onboarding process now embraces new HR technology, it's getting easier and more enjoyable for employees to start working for an organisation. With culture - and an employee's alignment with it - being vital for both parties, technology can play a significant part in creating that culture.

Recruiting employees that are of the right cultural fit for your organisation through technology is fast becoming commonplace. Having a real sense of the part an employee plays in an organisation not only helps them with their Ikigai, but it also helps the employer. The most engaged employees understand what part they play and how their daily work contributes to the success of the organisation.

Technology can encourage employees to act within their organisational values, collaborating and recognising each other's efforts. Understanding and living the values of the organisation is the key to developing a great employee experience.

Technology sits at the heart of the workplace, and forms a cornerstone of the employee experience. Almost eight per cent of executives rate the employee experience as, "very important" or "important". However, almost two thirds of executives say they aren't ready to address this new challenge[233]. The technology available to employers to help them improve the employee experience might be the best way to start tackling the problem. Changing our cultures and workplaces can take time and significant investment, whereas changing or improving workplace technology could be an easier and quicker way to improve the employee experience.

The pace of change in technology can leave employers to become irrelevant very quickly.

Forty-two per cent of Millennials[234] say they would quit a job that offered substandard technology and a massive 82 per cent said workplace technology influences even what role they would take[235]. As consumers, we can use the most up-to-date technology at home, but when we get to work, this stops. Americans' technology bills have now surpassed their heating bills as they spend more money on home technology than ever before[236]. This soaring popularity is having a detrimental effect on those organisations that fail to invest in, or adapt to, modern technology.

In the UK, many famous brands very quickly became bankrupt because of technology; Blockbuster, Kodak, Jessops, Borders, GAME – the list goes on. However, there are just as many success stories of those organisations that embraced modern technology, or diversified to accommodate it. Nokia famously started out by manufacturing wellington boots and other types of farm equipment. They moved into mobile phones after trying to find a way for farmers to communicate with each other across their land. PayPal, Google and Apple all started out as something very different to where they've ended up. They embraced changing attitudes to technology, and adapted to stay afloat. There has never been more competition for talent, and employers are finding it increasingly difficult to retain the best employees. Giving employees the ability to embrace the latest technologies to improve their productivity can make a difference. To see the impact of making minor changes to improve employees' overall success, we only need to look towards the Tour De France.

In 1903, the Tour De France started, and more than 100 years later, no British cyclist had ever won it. When Dave Brailsford became team director for the British Sky cycling team, he introduced the idea of the 'aggregation of marginal gains'. He believed that if he could improve every area related to cycling by just one per cent, those small gains would amount to a substantial improvement. The Sky team looked at everything they could do to improve their chances of winning; from supplements to better bikes and more streamlined clothing.

One of the most famous examples of Brailsford made small improvements to the Sky team was in the beds of the cyclists. In the Tour De France, the race takes place over 2,200 miles in 21 day-long segments. This means that cyclists are staying at different hotels along the course every night. Brailsford decided to ensure that each Sky cyclist was getting the best sleep they could every night – in the same bed. Sky arranged for a van to take each cyclist's bed ahead to the next hotel so that they could have a consistent and familiar night's sleep. To the surprise of many, it worked. In 2012, Sir Bradley Wiggins became the first British cyclist to win the Tour De France. That same year, Brailsford coached the British cycling team at the 2012 Olympic Games and won 70 per cent of all the gold medals available.

The removal of small frustrations, and the improvement in the technology we use every day can really help employees to improve their overall performance and productivity.

By making everything an employee must do within HR and reward easy to follow and understand, employers can improve employee satisfaction and productivity.

The Disney Corporation gives us a fitting example of how they've used technology to improve the employee experience. In 2005, Disney opened its first Disneyland in Hong Kong. Before each working day, Disney employees had to pick up their costumes from attendants. This meant that up to 3,000 employees could be picking up their costumes at the same time. This led to long queues, and a long wait before employees even started their shifts.

Being frustrated and tired is not the best way for anyone to start their day. So, Disney responded by implementing self-service kiosks. Employees can now arrive, scan their ID, pick up their costume and get to work[237]. The removal of this point of frustration meant employees could focus their energy on the working day ahead, and do it with a smile.

Within HR, technology spend must increase. If an employer's existing technology is old and difficult to use, employees simply won't use it. The demands on HR to do more with data means technology must be smart enough to gather it and present it in a useful format. As more and more employees search and apply for jobs online, there is an expectation that the whole onboarding process should be managed by technology.

HR is now able to pre-screen candidates using application tracking systems, and this is saving considerable time and cost. It's also helping to ensure that an employer's candidates have all the right skills and are a cultural fit – a must for creating the best workplace culture.

16. Innsaei

Iceland

Iceland is one of my favourite places in the world. I've been lucky enough to explore pretty much the entire island, and would even consider living there. As a country, the Icelandic culture is relaxed, intellectual, liberal, and peppered with folklore about elves and trolls (which most Icelanders still believe in). Within this rich history is an ancient language, and one word that's making a comeback is the word 'innsaei'. Innsaei has multiple meanings in Icelandic, but has no direct translation. The most common translations generally refer to 'The sea within' or 'Seeing from the inside out'. Innsaei refers to our inner world and feelings, and our intuition. In 2016, filmmaker Hrund Gunnsteinsdottir made a film about this old Icelandic word, called 'Innsaei'. Gunnsteinsdottir used to work at the UN but lost a connection with her work. She felt that she had started to serve a system, rather than people or the earth. The film explores how our rational, linear thinking has led to our ultimate disconnection from each other.

A great deal of research has been dedicated to how our decision-making is split between the brain's right and left hemispheres. While the left-hand brain is dominated by analytical processes, spatial information is processed on the right. Intuition is our ability to understand something and make decisions instinctively, without any cognitive reasoning.

The bridging of the gap between conscious and subconscious decision-making manifests itself physically as a sensation that appears quickly like a gut feeling or a 'hunch'.

When I was about 24 years old, I travelled around Morocco for a few weeks and one of the most inspiring and memorable moments of my life came from lying on the Sahara Desert, looking up at the stars. That night, in my best French (and in his best English) I tried to talk to a Nomad who had led us into the desert. I asked him how he could navigate back to his family within the depths of the desert without any navigation equipment once the Summer tourist season had ended. From what I could translate, he told me intuition and the stars were all he needed. In the film 'Innsaei', a similar story of how Polynesian navigators sailed ships around the world using only their experiences and intuition is regaled.

There are many occasions at work when we might feel uneasy about an event. A deal might seem suspicious, a colleague might not seem genuine, but every time, without knowing why, we felt something was wrong deep in our gut. This intuition is a lot more than just an old wives' tale, and it might help us perform better at work. Intuition has been subjected to a lot of attention by the scientific community, as many psychologists believe our subconscious acts so accurately and quickly, even our best guesses aren't guesses at all. One study sought to prove this by studying car buyers[238].

They monitored buyers who had plenty of time to mull over their car-buying process, and others who had to make a quick purchasing decision. The researchers found that those who could read lots of info about their choice of car, and think long and hard about the purchase were found to be satisfied with their purchase just 25 per cent of the time. This was compared to 60 per cent for those who made an impulse decision.

Researchers have considered how people's quick decisions are usually better than those that are given a lot of thought. Experts believe this is because of the Sherlock-style assessment we subconsciously give to situations that help our decision-making. It was once described to me as, "the feeling you get when you walk into a familiar place like your living room, and you're able to know that someone has been in the room". Our brains recognise so much of the room; the light, the objects in it, where they're usually placed etc., that the smallest change is registered in our subconscious, and we know something has changed. Joel Person and colleagues from the School of Psychology at the University of New South Wales conducted a study into how we can measure intuition. Their findings supported the idea of human intuition[239] and many more have mirrored the results.

One of the first business books I ever remember reading was Jonah Lehrer's The Decisive Moment. It's a fascinating book which I couldn't put down for days. It played perfectly into a time in my life when my psychology degree started to become very useful in the workplace.

In the book, Lehrer looked at how we make decisions and whether we should trust our gut. The book explores how our rational and unconscious minds work. Lehrer believes that our unconscious mind can process more informational than our rational, thinking mind. Just like my example of entering a familiar room, Lehrer found the same feeling when he studied the British Navy.

During the Gulf War, British Navy radar operator Michael Riley noticed a blip on his radar that he identified as an enemy missile heading straight towards him. He fired two missiles in response, and single-handedly saved USS Missouri from attack. However, the blip of an enemy missile and the blip of an American fighter jet look the same on radar. Riley could have blown up an American plane. Two years after everyone thought Riley was just lucky, cognitive psychologist Gary Klein reviewed the radar tapes, and found something a lot more complex than just luck. Klein found that Michael Riley only ever detected radar over the sea and was familiar with seeing American fighter jets flying over from Kuwait. As the missile flew at a lower altitude, its signal didn't show up on radar until slightly later than that of a fighter jet would. This small, eight-second difference was enough to tell Riley's subconscious that this signal was different to what he was used to seeing and gave him an uneasy feeling. All while he had no conscious knowledge of what his body was processing.

Using our intuition at work might be a way of saving time and producing better results.

Robin Hogarth from the ICREA and Pompeu Fabra University in Barcelona examined the benefits of making decisions analytically and trusting our intuition[240]. Hogarth suggests that mastering the balance between when to use more thought-out decision-making, and when to trust our instincts is a skill we could all benefit from.

In one study, Deciding Advantageously Before Knowing the Advantageous Strategy[241], researchers asked participants to play a card game to win the most money. Participants were asked to choose from two sets of cards; one was set up to give big wins followed by big losses, and the other set would give small gains, but little losses. It took around 50 turns of a card before the participants started to get a hunch that one deck was better than the other, and a further 30 cards before they could tell the difference. However, what the researchers discovered was that after only 10 draws of a card, the participants' physiology started to change. The participants' hands sweated more every time they reached for the losing deck. Long before the brain could notice that there was a difference, the body was able to tell. In similar studies, people have shown an amazing ability to recognise and predict patterns in their bodies before their brains could[242].

The manner and speed at which our bodies process information is amazing. The fact that the body can do it all so quickly before the mind can catch up is even more remarkable. Researchers from Boston College's School of Management examined the links between subject matter expertise and intuitive decision-making[243].

In one of their tests, the researchers asked participants to decide whether a designer handbag was genuine or fake. Among those participants who owned several luxury-branded bags, they could make quicker and more effective decisions about the origin of the bags. Their exposure to - and knowledge of - the subject matter made their intuitive decisions more accurate. What is interesting about intuition is that it doesn't require any conscious rational thinking.

As we've seen in the car-buying experiment, too much time and information can impede our decision-making abilities. Shabnam Mousavi from the John Hopkins Carey Business School in Washington D.C. examined Heuristics[244]. Heuristics is an approach that encourages people to solve problems faster without doing all the thinking we usually would. Heuristics are like cognitive shortcuts that help us simplify decisions. In her research, Mousavi asked both German and US students which city was larger: Detroit or Milwaukee. She found that 90 per cent of the Germans got the question right when only 60 per cent of the Americans did. Mousavi found the German students had simply picked the city with the most familiar name, assuming it was familiar because it was the largest. The American students had good knowledge of the overall country and over-thought the answer, and ultimately most got it wrong.

Instinctive decision-making has benefits when a decision needs to be made quickly, but researchers also suggest that senior managers should reinforce employees' use of intuition in other situations[245].

Incorporating intuition into decision-making can help when decisions needs to be made that are consistent with an organisation's culture and values.

Allowing and encouraging employees to use their intuition at work is enforcing our trust in their abilities and experience. Many researchers agree that the importance of intuition cannot be ignored[246].

17. Ras-le-bol

France

As technology quickly advances the workplace, it brings huge benefits. However, many years on, some technology is having the opposite effect. On average, we receive 304 business emails a week and check our email accounts 36 times an hour[247]. Email has become a significant distraction at work, and the French have 'ras-le-bol'. The phrase doesn't have a direct translation, but roughly means 'had enough' or 'had it up to here'. The phrase perfectly sums up many employees' despair at the prevalence of email, and as a result, many organisations are now starting to look to other ways to communicate. Six in 10 American workers say that email is 'very important' to them[248]. Our reliance on this intrusive technology might be getting too much.

Barack Obama famously banned all smartphones from Cabinet meetings at the White House. Obama felt phones were a distraction, as employees constantly checked emails and texts. As technology continues to dominate our lives, there is a growing need to 'switch off' from this over-indulgence. Film director Christopher Nolan has also imposed a strict no-phone policy on his sets. In Esquire magazine, Nolan spoke to Adam Grant, PhD, Professor of Organisational Psychology from University of Pennsylvania's Wharton School.

He explained that he didn't let people have phones on set because people think they're better at multitasking than they actually are[249].

After worldwide media attention, the French became the trailblazers in this new way of thinking when they passed a law commonly referred to as the 'Right to disconnect'. To restore a decent work-life balance for employees, French companies with more than 50 employees are now required to give their workers the 'right to disconnect' when they leave their workplace. Those who support this new law think that employees who are expected to check and reply to work emails outside of normal working hours are exposed to higher risk of stress and burnout. Peter Jenkinson, Business Development Director at Wrkit, feels just as passionate about enabling this disconnect from work. "Let's stop it! Turn it off! Discourage - even disallow - employees from sending emails outside of working hours. Then, sit back and watch; not only will the company not implode, but employee health and performance will improve".

In a leading new piece of research, psychologists Larissa Barber and Alecia Santuzzi examined how employees feel the urge to respond quickly to emails outside of work[250]. They referred to this experience as 'telepressure'. The research revealed that telepressure in the workplace is now a predictor of employee burnout, absenteeism, and sleep quality. Barber and Santuzzi concluded that those organisations that have put measures in place to prevent employees from responding to emails outside of working hours have seen positive results.

They recommend that more employers consider adopting technology use policies, or providing training to help employees set boundaries.

The science behind why we use our smartphones and the internet so much is starting to be considered by researchers. In their report A Nation Addicted to Smartphones, the British regulator Ofcom revealed that over a quarter of adults and nearly half of all teenagers now own a smartphone[251]. Thirty-seven per cent of adults and 60 per cent of teenagers classed themselves as being 'highly addicted' to their smartphones, and this addiction is starting to affect their social behaviour. Ofcom found that the clear majority of smartphone users in the UK (81 per cent) leave their phone switched on all the time - even when they are in bed. We already know that the lines between work and home life are growing increasingly blurred, and the Ofcom report has confirmed this. More than 30 per cent of smartphone users say they regularly take part in personal calls during worktime, but they also admit to taking work calls while on annual leave[252]. A work/life balance no longer exists – the two are now entwined.

When Obama banned smartphones from White House meetings, he wouldn't even let the phones be taken into the room. It seems he was onto something new, as research suggests that just the mere presence of our smartphones can affect our brains. The McCombs School of Business at the University of Texas conducted experiments with almost 800 smartphone users to see how well they could complete tasks when their smartphones were near, but weren't being used[253].

The researchers selected random participants to put their smartphones face-down on their desk, put away in their bag or in another room. The researchers then tested the participants. They found that just being close to their smartphones reduced the participants' cognitive capacity, and even impaired their cognitive functions. Just having our phones within easy reach is enough to distract us to perform worse at a task.

The University of California, Irvine, found that the average office worker is interrupted every three minutes and five seconds[254]. They found that employees compensate for these interruptions by working faster, which results in increased stress and frustration. One of the biggest interruptions to our lives in the 21st century is the ping of a notification from our smartphones. Our social media channels, emails, text messages etc. are all designed to draw us back to our phone as different apps compete for our attention.

The prevalence of smartphones is also having a negative effect on our physical health. Almost half of Brits report walking into something because of being fixated on their smartphone screens while walking[255]. These distractions are even enough to kill people[256]. Alarmingly, we are even seeing an increase in poor eyesight because of how often we use screens. By 2050, it's estimated that 50 per cent of the entire world will need glasses as a direct result of using screens too much[257]. As more and more employees use their phones at work, we are also seeing the surprising effects of everyday social media use on our health.

Two thirds of people in the UK report 'feeling inferior' after seeing the wealth and experiences of friends and celebrities on social media[258]. More than one third of Brits have also admitted to taking a break from social media, or deleting their accounts altogether to improve their mental health.

The worst social networking site for young people's mental health is reported to be Instagram[259]. Users sharing photographs of luxury goods, long-haul vacations, and attractive people is leading to feelings of inadequacy and anxiety. Some experts suggest that having a social media curfew for just a few hours every day can make us happier. Work might be the best time to encourage this period of switching off, and will allow employees to focus more on the present and those around them.

Comedian and presenter Bill Maher has likened our addiction with social media to smoking. Maher has called on tech social media giants to "admit they're just tobacco farmers in T-shirts selling an addictive product to children". In the Journal of Cyberpsychology, Behavior and Social Networking, a group of researchers examined the impact social media was having on us. They found that just seeing the Facebook logo is enough to make us want to log in – even if it's for less than a second[260].

Our addiction to smartphones has become so prevalent that one addiction therapist has said that giving a child a smartphone is like "giving them a gram of cocaine"[261].

Mandy Saligari who heads the Harley Street Charter clinic in London says children as young as 13 years old are being treated for technology addiction in the UK.

The 2013 Mobile Consumer Habits study reveals that people admit using their phones while having sex (9 per cent), in the shower (12 per cent) and even while driving (55 per cent)[262]. Leonid Miakotko has studied the effect smartphones are having on our health[263]. He noted that extensive users of smartphones report discomfort in at least one area of their upper back or neck. Mikakotko cites research by Balakrishnan and Chinnavan who say, "prolonged use of cell phones is known to cause symptoms of musculoskeletal disorder. Keeping this into consideration, more studies should be done in the future to create awareness among smartphone users regarding the seriousness of this matter".

Gloria Mark from the University of California discovered that for every 30 seconds we are distracted, we lose 30 minutes of concentration[264]. It then takes us half an hour to re-focus on the original task we were doing. When we stop to respond to an email, our minds get so distracted that we need to take even more time to get back into what we were doing. Checking emails takes up a massive 28 per cent of an employee's time[265]. The average office worker sends more than 100 emails a day[266]. In a classroom setting, technology has been shown to distract children to the extent that those classrooms that banned laptops and tablets showed higher results than those that permitted them[267].

There is a growing need for employees to find time to switch off from their emails, phones and the internet. Meetings offer employees an opportunity to connect with colleagues, clients, and suppliers. This time might be an ideal way to disconnect employees from phones and emails and focus on interacting with their colleagues.

18. Auszeit

Austria

In Austria, lots of auszeit, or 'time off', is something that is encouraged more than anywhere else in the world. According to statistics from the International Labour Organisation, Austrian employees get 13 paid public holidays every year on top of the statutory minimum 25 days' vacation[268]. This gives Austrian employees around 38 days off work every year – among the highest in the world. Despite many countries offering decent levels of vacation allowance, research reveals that employees are still not taking advantage of what is on offer. It's reported that a third of UK and 25 per cent of US employees don't take all their vacation entitlement. According to the CIPD[269], data from more than 1,000 employees reveals that a further 15 per cent of UK employees only take their entitlement of annual leave because their employer makes them.

The growing trend to be 'always on' at work means that taking time off is now more important to employees than ever before. Work-related stress, anxiety and depression are on the rise, and both employees and employers need to take responsibility for it. Research signals that this is a worrying trait for younger workers especially. Project Time Off reveals that Millennials are not just not taking the vacation they earn, they're also the most likely to forfeit time off[270].

Worrying about their manager's opinion of them and concerned with being replaced is leading the youngest workers to risk burnout. In the UK, many employees are at substantial risk of burnout, as despite relatively generous vacation allowances, more than a third are working an extra 13 days a year with more than half admitting they work more than their contracted hours[271]. An alarming 10 per cent of UK employees work every single day of the week.

Research published in the Applied Research in Quality of Life Journal[272] has considered the association between vacations and a person's happiness. Researchers compared the happiness of those people who went on vacation with those who didn't. More than 1,500 Dutch people took part in the study about their happiness before and after taking a trip. Those people who took a vacation reported higher happiness before the trip than those who didn't take a vacation. This study showed no difference between post-vacation happiness in either group. What this study suggests is that looking forward to a vacation increases an employee's happiness before they even go away.

Having a vacation to look forward to appears to create double benefits for employees. Not only do they get the time away from work for respite, they also benefit from the good feeling associated with looking forward to their vacation.

The author Gretchen Rubin states that there are four stages for enjoying an event like a vacation: anticipation, savouring, expression and reflection. One of the most surprising stages is that anticipation of a vacation alone brings happiness into employee's lives. Sometimes, that anticipation can lead to feeling happier than even doing the thing you are looking forward to.

This feeling was famously noted by Winnie the Pooh author, A. A. Milne when he wrote, '"well," said Pooh, "what I like best," and then he had to stop and think. Because although Eating Honey was a very good thing to do, there was a moment just before you began to eat it which was better than when you were, but he didn't know what it was called.' Psychologists refer to this as feeling as 'Rosy prospection'[273]. Employers can tap into this feeling by encouraging employees to spend their time off work doing enjoyable activities.

The absence of a regular vacation can have a profound effect on our bodies. A study that investigated the reasons behind myocardial infraction or coronary death among women found that (among other things), infrequent vacations are a predictor of ill health[274]. Similar studies have also found that vacations can reduce the adverse effects of stress on physical and mental health. A study by Gerhard Strauss-Blasche et al[275] looked at the impact of vacation time on stress. Their results indicated that a restful vacation may act as a buffer for work-related stress.

The positive impact of vacation time has clear benefits for the individual concerned.

However, it may also benefit those around them, as research points to vacation time promoting better quality relationships with those people who surround us, including our co-workers. A 2013 study by Sweden's Uppsala University[276] found that vacations enable people to help each other and renew relationships. The researchers found that the benefits of vacations can even be felt by those people we have chance encounters with, like strangers in a coffee shop and most importantly for employers, their customers. The positive feelings associated with vacations can help to make employees happier at work.

American employees are half as likely to go on a vacation overseas than European employees[277]. Experiencing and learning from new cultures is really what this book is all about. But travelling in general can have huge benefits for employees. A joint study between the Global Commission on Ageing and Transamerica Center for Retirement Studies and the U.S. Travel Association revealed that travelling abroad can actually improve our health. The study found that women who vacation at least twice a year showed significantly lower risk of suffering heart attacks than those women who only travelled every six years or less[278]. Experiencing new cultures and thinking in a different way are all by-products of travelling that create new neural connections in our brains. These new neural connections can improve our logic and problem-solving skills[279].

But travelling can also make happier employees in general. As we've seen, as well as experiencing new things, the anticipation alone is enough to make employees happier[280].

A well-studied concept in psychology is something called 'overcommitment'. Psychologists believe that overcommitment is a product of 'poor limit-setting' and is often found in employees where they find setting boundaries at work challenging. One of the negative effects of an over-engaged employee is overcommitment. We'll all recognise these employees as the ones who find it difficult to say "no" when they're asked for help at work. We often see overcommitment in high-performing employees who will often jump in and solve a problem at work as soon as they see it, even when it's not their problem to solve. The impact overcommitment has on employees has been examined as 'high-effort, low-reward', and can adversely affect the health of men, according to one study[281].

Some organisations are taking employee overcommitment so seriously, its become a sackable offence. In October 2017, supermarket Lidl fired one of its Barcelona managers for working too hard[282]. The supermarket fired the manager for "very serious laboural unfulfillment" after he was spotted on CCTV coming in early and working on his own (both actions against company policy). Setting boundaries between home and work life is not just about health, it's also about being able to maintain healthy relationships outside of work. We require time to recover from work, and taking a vacation is a perfect opportunity for us to switch off completely.

Nine of the top 10 most productive countries measured by GDP per hour worked are all European[283]. Europe also has some of the most generous annual vacation allowances in the world.

In the USA, a staggering 54 per cent of American employees don't use their full vacation entitlement, and this is resulting in more than 600 million unused vacation days across the country. That's a massive $236 billion lost in total spending[284]. Employees who take their vacation entitlement are also financially better off. According to the study Project: Time Off, employees who take 11 days or more annual vacation are more likely to get a pay rise or promotion than those who take 10 or fewer[285].

Taking time not just away from the office, but away from everyday life can improve the lives of employees. Psychology says it can also improve our ability to problem solve[286], so should be as important to employers as it is to employees.

19. Karoshi

Japan

Karoshi is roughly translated as 'overwork death' in Japanese. It refers to the sudden death of someone at work. Typically, these are heart attacks and stress-related fatalities, and they're a very real problem. The world's media has reported a lot in recent years about the culture in Japan that has caused many to work overtime and, in extreme cases, this overworking has led to employee deaths. In the most recent case to grab the media's attention, Miwa Sado, a 31-year-old journalist died in 2013 from heart failure[287]. She had just completed 159 hours of overtime.

Large advertising agency, Dentsu, have been one of the organisations in the spotlight after excessive overtime demands came to light. Similarly, the sad story of Joey Tocnang's fate gave a very real face to the growing phenomenon. The 27-year-old casting company trainee died of heart failure, and the inquest revealed his death was directly linked to the long hours of overtime he was forced to undertake. Japan's Government has warned that 20 per cent of the entire workforce is at risk of death from overworking[288].

The high productivity and economic output of Asian organisations in general has impressed the world for a long time, but is coming at a cost.

In Singapore and Hong Kong, the annual absence rate per employee is 54 and 70 days respectively[289]. The long hours and longer weeks are taking their toll on Japanese employees in particular. The Japanese Government is intervening to stop this negative work culture, and big business is starting to deal with large compensation claims related to Karoshi. There is now a growing trend to alleviate worker stress in Japan. Where some organisations are taking small steps to correct this culture, others are taking more drastic steps.

The benefits of a shorter working week have long been debated across the world, but as the lines between home and work blur more than ever before, some recognise the need to address this. In early 2017, Yahoo Japan Corp announced it was considering reducing working days to just four days a week by 2020[290]. A Yahoo Japan Corp spokeswoman told RT News, "by giving employees more freedom on how to work, we're hoping that employees choose a style that lets them perform at their best, so that we boost productivity". The Government has even supported a strategy called 'Premium Friday' where employees are encouraged to leave at 3pm on a Friday.

When we consider the traditional working week across the world, we think of five days of eight hours. However, research is showing that everywhere (not just Japan), people are frequently working more than those eight hours a day. Research shows that more than 50 per cent of full-time employees spend more than 40 hours per week at the office[291].

Employees who work long hours or are overworked are more likely to suffer serious health issues including heart attacks, diabetes and strokes. Ultimately, it's not just the employee who will pay for this overworking, but employers, as productivity declines and healthcare costs increase significantly.

We've already looked at the importance of sleep in enabling employees to perform at their best, and it's clear that those working longer hours have less sleep than others. Working long hours leaves little time to wind down after work, and the result is poor sleep patterns among those who work too much. Nick Court, Founder and CEO of Cloud9 People, told me, "many industries suffer from presenteeism, and some of this is because they value time at the desk rather than the output from individuals and teams. As the main contractual transaction between employer and employee is based around time, this is unsurprising". Court thinks if organisations start to value output, this can change the working relationship. "The employee may still need to be on-site for the full working day, but the pace they set is up to them. This is a more adult relationship and requires trust in the employee".

In the US, the state of Utah implemented a three-day weekend for all state-employed workers. They discovered after just 10 months, they saved $1.8 million in energy costs. Other organisations have seen unauthorised absences reduce, and overall productivity increased by implementing a three-day weekend.

A three-day weekend is fast becoming a unique selling point for employees too, as more working parents are becoming employed. Offering employees a more flexible working pattern can be a big pull. The desire to have more flexible working patterns has been seen in the rise of the gig economy. The number of 'on demand' workers is expected to double in the next four years. This will result in more than nine million Americans working in the gig economy by 2021[292].

There is a lot of science backing the idea of giving employees longer weekends. In fact, research from psychologists and the medical profession overwhelmingly back the idea of a three-day weekend or a shorter working week. In 2015, The Lancet[293] published a large analysis of studies in this area. They concluded that employees who work longer hours had a 33 per cent increased risk of a stroke than others[294].

In the UK, the topic has also been getting more attention, as one of the major political parties adds a three-day weekend to its manifesto. In early 2017, the Green Party proposed the idea since so many Brits are already working 10-hour days anyway. Whatever your opinion of a shorter working week or a longer weekend, one thing is for sure – we aren't as productive as we used to be. Productivity growth has steadily declined since 1975 and it's holding our economy back. The UK is technically at full employment, so we can't get more people to do the job, which means we need to switch tactics. Something must change, and we can't just get people to work longer hours.

As we've already read in this book, the longer someone works, the less productive they are.

A shorter working week has shown to have specific benefits for older workers. As the average age of retirement continues to get higher and higher, strategies that benefit older employees should be considered by employers. A report published by the Melbourne Institute Worker Paper[295] series looked at the performance of men and women over the course of a working week. The researchers studied 3,000 men and 3,500 women. They discovered that the cognitive performance of middle-aged men improved as the working week progressed, but only up to 25 hours a week. As the week went over 25 hours, overall performance decreased as fatigue and stress started to kick in. The researchers concluded that for those employees over the age of 40, there were benefits of a shorter working week as these employees were not performing at their best after they had reached the week's half-way point.

Compared to 20 years ago, employees are twice as likely to report that they are exhausted at work. More than half of employees report that they are often or always exhausted because of work[296]. This burnout is causing employees serious health problems, and is even leading to loneliness. The isolation some employees feel because of working too much or feeling exhausted could be having a huge negative impact on their lives. Research has even gone as far as to state that too much work is shortening our lives – by a whopping 70 per cent[297].

There is a new concept in the world of work that could help employers with implementing a shorter working week and avoiding overwork.

It's called the Results Only Work Environment (ROWE). The concept of ROWE was developed by Cali Ressler and Jody Thompson. They first published this approach in their book, Why Work Sucks and How to Fix it. ROWE measures an employee or team performance by output only, and not where they work or for how long. Research is split over the impact of ROWE, and results vary from organisation to organisation. However, early results have shown that the organisational benefits to implementing ROWE could be significant.

Some of the benefits of ROWE include the positive impacts it has on employee sleep duration, self-reported health and energy levels. There have also been reports of increased job satisfaction, organisational commitment, and a reduction in employee turnover. However, the organisation that most famously implemented ROWE, later abandoned it. Best Buy initially reported saving $2.2 million by implementing ROWE, but as the company struggled financially, an investment in a longer-term strategy was replaced by one that delivered immediate cost savings[298].

In a well-known case study of ROWE by CultureRX, the clothing retailer Gap chose to implement it and called it, "a cultural revolution"[299].

With more than 132,000 global employees across 3,000 stores, Gap recognised several problems they needed to address including the work/life balance of their employees. Giving Gap employees the autonomy to work from where they needed to (or preferred to), was going to offer clear benefits to those feeling the stress of work or home life. Just after the initial pilot, 75 per cent of Gap employees said the ROWE model was the most special aspect of Gap's working environment. Productivity increased by 17 per cent, quality of work increased by 23 per cent, and even service levels improved by two per cent. Gap understood that the wellbeing of their employees was going to be vital to their continued operational success, and the new work/life balance resulted in a new corporate motto; "Better You. Better Gap". Implementation of ROWE within an organisation has even been suggested to close the gender pay gap as the lives of working mothers can become easier[300].

Employees are leaving work, going home and barely resting before going to work again. For many, this cycle of work and little rest has led to a reduction in social connections, as work dominates their lives. Some experts are so concerned with our fixation on the working day, that alternatives to ROWE and the 9-to-5 are being suggested regularly. HR Grapevine reports a new theory by Neville Henderson of Pasfield Curran; annualised working hours[301]. Whatever methods employers consider, it's clear that giving employees the opportunity to spend more time with their social circles can have huge benefits to their own wellbeing as well as the quality of their work.

Improving our social connections has been proven to strengthen our immune system and reduce our chances of becoming depressed[302].

Taking a new view of how and when we work might just be the secret to improving working conditions for employees, and increasing output for employers. Enabling employees to work from home can allow them to spend more time with their family by removing long commutes and adding more time to their days. Reducing the number of working days enables all employees to benefit from more social time and improve their overall mental health. Creating an environment where employees are feeling fulfilled and happy can only be a good thing for an employer and their customers.

20. Music

UK

I'm an enthusiastic fan of music. I listen to it whenever I can. I go to sleep listening to music, I drive listening to music, I sit on the train listening to music and, more importantly, I frequently work while listening to music. I've often wondered how music can impact our ability to do our jobs. It's well known that music can alter our mood, and retailers and filmmakers are all quite adept at using it to their advantage[303].

A recent British study on the effects of music used opioid blockers to measure the impact[304]. Opioid blockers interfere with the brain's ability to feel pleasure. Researchers gave opioids to half of their participants, and gave the other half a placebo. They then had both groups listen to music. Those who had taken the opioids enjoyed the music much less than the placebo group. They concluded that music has a similar effect on our brains as food and drugs do.

Many studies have shown that listening to music can induce feelings of pleasure. Interestingly, people frequently rank music as one of the top 10 things that gives them pleasure in life, but can listening to music make us work any better? Psychologist Maria Witek reveals that there is a specific type of music that we need to be listening to: groove music[305].

The music must be upbeat enough to get us in the right mood, but not so much that it makes us want to dance. Researchers cite James Brown as the ideal type of music to lift our mood. Using music to encourage a more upbeat atmosphere in work would clearly have its benefits, but can music help employees focus more?

Music can provide us with a consistent and neutral background noise. Freeing ourselves from loud noises, other people's conversations, and other distractions can help us to focus on the task at hand. In 1972, a now famous study looked at the impact music had on workers in a factory[306]. The results supported the idea that music was effective in raising efficiency in factory workers. Part of the reason was that the negative effects of the loud machinery were countered by music.

What type of music you listen to can influence how you feel. However, it can also have an effect depending on what type of work you are trying to do. Specifically, if you're trying to read, music has a negative effect. If you want to encourage your employees to work harder and concentrate more, they need to be listening to instrumental music.

When we listen to music with lyrics, our brains try to digest and understand what we are listening to. Listening to music without any lyrics gives us the ability to block out unwelcome noises and distractions, without giving our mind additional information to process.

Psychologists refer to this type of music as 'low information load'. Rauscher, Shaw and Ky conducted an experiment in 1994 that looked at the impacts of listening to Mozart. They discovered that this type of music increased spatial reasoning in college students. This has become commonly known as 'The Mozart Effect'[307]. Since this initial study, many people now use classical music like Mozart, to help them study and learn.

Despite its initial fame, The Mozart Effect has been heavily criticised over the years, as many question the original results. However, what the initial study did do is prompt a wealth of others to examine how music can improve our cognitive abilities. A 2011 a British study looked at employees who listened to a personal electronic device (like an iPhone) while they worked[308]. Nearly 300 employees were studied, and the researchers identified several new benefits to listening to music while working. Inspiration, concentration, stress relief, and the ability to effectively manage personal space were all improved when an employee listened to personal music. The researchers found that music enabled employees to 'seal themselves off' from the office environment, which - as we'll see in the next chapter - can have huge benefits to our productivity. Some researchers have even gone as far as to study specific songs to find out which well-known tunes can impact us psychologically.

Cognitive Neuroscientist Dr Jacob Jolij commissioned a UK survey to see what songs improved our mood the most.

Looking at tempo and lyrics, Jolij discovered that Queen's 'Don't Stop Me Now', ABBA's 'Dancing Queen', The Beach Boys' 'Good Vibrations', Billy Joel's 'Uptown Girl', and Survivor's 'Eye of the Tiger' were the top five songs to improve our mood[309]. Other research into the specific types of music we should be listening to points to Koan music (music typically used for meditating). Listening to Koan music has been shown to produce better results than not listening to any music at all[310].

As well as improving our ability to concentrate and be more productive, music can also make us happier. Researchers have shown that listening to happy music is an effective way to improve our mood. In their research, If You're Happy and You Know It: Music Engagement and Subjective Wellbeing, researchers Melissa K. Weinberg and Dawn Joseph explored the connection between music engagement and wellbeing[311]. They found that engaging with music in the company of others improved the subject's wellbeing. Using music to improve an employee's wellbeing might have more significant effects than we think. Music has been found to prevent anxiety[312] and in one study, it's even shown to be more powerful than medicine. Bringman et al[313] studied the effects of music on patients who had undergone hernia repair. They found that those patients who listened to music following surgery require less morphine to relieve pain that those who hadn't.

Music has also been seen to reduce the pain suffered by people with fibromyalgia[314].

As well as relieving pain, listening to music could also help employees improve their immune systems. Researchers at Wilkes University examined how listening to music can affect levels of Immunoglobulin (IgA). They found that those who had been exposed to soothing music had significantly larger increases in IgA[315]. IgA is an antibody that plays a primary role in the immune functions.

Some researchers have considered the impact music can have on tasks that require concentration, like driving. Listening to music while driving was thought to have a negative impact, but it actually has positive effects too. In one study, subjects' mood was improved, and they displayed a more relaxed body state when listening to music while driving[316]. Music can improve our driving ability by improving our coordination skills[317]. Music has also been found to enhance our reaction times[318], so encouraging music for those employees who drive as part of their work should be considered.

Allowing employees to listen to music at work could be a simple and effective way to not just improve their mood and productivity, but also their perception of the workplace. More than half of HR professionals believe that music is a motivational tool in the workplace[319]. Research by LinkedIn and Spotify reveals that office music has a calming effect on half of HR professionals and helped 40 per cent to be more creative. Although scientists aren't quite sure why we like music so much, it's clear that we form an emotional connection with it.

This connection can be so strong, it can alter our visual perceptions. One study has shown that music can make happy faces appear happier[320].

21. Bürolandschaft

Germany

Bürolandschaft was a German movement in the 1950s, aimed at 'opening up' workplaces to install open plan offices. Bürolandschaft was designed to encourage egalitarian management as well as creating an environment that would produce more communication and collaborative working.

During the 1950s and 60s, the socialist values that were sweeping across Europe at the time led to the creation of this new office trend. Managers were no longer locked away in private offices, and workers were no longer constrained to partitioned desks in rows. As embraced as the trend was, and still is (70 per cent of all offices have an open floor plan[321]), research suggests that nowadays, it's doing the opposite of what was first intended.

Almost half of American workers don't like their physical work environment[322]. Open plan offices have made it much easier for employees to be distracted. An employee's proximity to their colleagues is giving them too much communication and spontaneous meetings/conversations are eating away at productivity. Open plan offices also prevent us from focusing. A 2012 study by Gensler surveyed 90,000 people about how they work[323].

They found that since 2007, the less space, privacy and time we have, combined with more distractions, are making our ability to focus at work more time-consuming than ever before. Where we work is an area of much debate in the modern workplace, as technology enables us to move away from the office more often.

Where we do our work is becoming more and more influential on an employee's ability to do their job and enjoy it. Abdul Raziq and Raheela Maulabakhsh have considered the impact our working environment has on our job satisfaction[324]. They studied educational institutions, banking, and telecommunication employers in Pakistan. Their results indicated that there was a direct relationship between employee satisfaction and their working environment. Raziq and Maulabakhsh suggest that employers need to understand the influence of a good working environment on the overall success of their employees. Despite results like these, almost half of global employees say their workplace stops them from working productively[325].

The researchers allowed employees to decorate their workplace however they liked, with as many pictures and plants as they wanted. When they compared the results of workers' productivity after they had created their own spaces, they found that employees were 32 per cent more productive when working in the space they created themselves[326]. Google really locked in on what their employees needed when they built their famous New York campus. No part of the office is said to be more than 150 feet away from food.

This is to encourage employees to snack and eat in such a way that encourages them to interact with each other and remain at their workstations for longer.

We've already touched on the features of Feng Shui in the workplace earlier in this book when we looked at the benefits of fresh air. Small improvements like adding plants to an office can help to reduce pollution, but also lower employee stress levels[327]. In fact, increasing the presence of the colour green alone has advantages. We process the colour green much more easily than any other colour. It's also been shown to enhance performance on tasks that generate innovative ideas[328]. People associate the colour green with a feeling of calmness, happiness, comfort and peace[329]. Maybe it's time your office had a green face lift?

Unwanted noise and background noise especially can be a big distraction. A 2013 study by Klatte, Bergstrom and Lachmann[330] looked at the effect of noise on children's ability to learn. Lachmann et al discovered that indoor noise and reverberation in classroom settings were associated with poorer verbal performance in children[331]. Noise can be a distraction and so psychology has devoted a lot of research into how can impede us. From aircraft noise affecting our ability to read, to background music improving performance, more than three quarters of employees prefer to work in the quiet, and a third are dissatisfied with the noise levels in their primary workspace[332].

It is said that humans can only listen to 1.6 conversations at a time[333].

An open plan office gives us the ability to overhear close-by conversations on the phone or in person, and these take up some of our brain capacity. In the Journal of Environmental Psychology[334], Aram Seddigh and colleagues looked specifically at the effect of the noise of an open plan office on employees. The researchers took two floors of an office building and manipulated the acoustics. Their results showed that on either floor, enhancing the acoustics resulted in lower perceived disturbances, and participants reported lower cognitive stress. The researchers also revealed that even a small deterioration in the acoustics of an open plan office had a negative impact on the participants' self-rated health and disturbances.

In 2002, researchers conducted a longitudinal study within a large private oil and gas company to see how the design of their workplace affected their employees[335]. They assessed the employees' satisfaction with the physical environment, physical stress, co-worker relations, and perceived job performance. Using a sample of 21 employees, researchers surveyed them before and after their workplace went from a traditional office to an open plan one. After six months of the changes, employees reported a drop in almost every measure. They found the new office layout to be disruptive and stressful. Unsurprisingly, productivity also fell.

Many home and remote workers claim they're more productive when at home. No watercooler moments, no distracting conversations and no ad-hoc meetings.

Researchers at Exeter University found that employees who were given the opportunity to arrange an office how they wanted were 32 per cent more productive[336]. The privacy aspect of working from home could lead to higher productivity, too. In their examination of numerous studies, researchers from the University of Tennessee at Knoxville, looked at the relationship between architectural privacy, psychological privacy, and job satisfaction and performance[337]. They found that any kind of privacy was associated with higher employee satisfaction.

According to one study, the open plan office and its subsequent noise is making us even more stressed. Gary Evans and Dana Johnson published research in the Journal of Occupational Psychology that suggest the background noise of an open plan office demotivates employees[338].

As well as a reduction in productivity and motivation, it's also thought that the open plan office can contribute to sickness absence. One study looked at a national survey of Danish people working in offices. They found that an employee's sickness absence was significantly related to having a greater number of occupants in their office. Employees working in open plan offices had 62 per cent more sick days than those in smaller, cellular offices[339].

Choosing where we work could hugely benefit our ability to concentrate and be productive. Research suggests that those sitting near us can also have an influence. Specifically, if we want to be more productive, we must sit next to someone who is already productive.

The Harvard Business Review looked at data from more than 2,000 employees in the US and Europe[340]. The researchers measured workers' productivity, effectiveness, and quality of work. They then examined the impact the 'office neighbours' had on an employee's performance, and found that the neighbours' influence was significant. Researchers at the Harvard Business Review[341] found that the seating patterns of certain personalities impacted both workers positively. When productive workers sat next to quality workers, there was a 13 per cent increase in productivity. However, the impact of inferior quality employees was just as significant. Toxic workers (those who ended up being fired for their behaviour) negatively influenced their neighbour's performance. They even found that sitting toxic employees close to each other increased the chances of one of them being fired by a massive 27 per cent.

As the act of simply sitting at a desk is beginning to be heavily criticised, we need to drastically redesign the common office. The sheer amount of time we spend sitting down each day has been referred to as "the new smoking", and many predict similar lawsuits to those aimed at cigarettes manufacturers aren't far behind[342]. Whatever your preference, employees should be able to choose a workplace and way of working that fits in with their own personality. If they are producing results, where an employee works is no longer important.

22. Keluarga

Indonesia

Keluarga means 'family' in Indonesian. Indonesia is the largest Muslim country in the world, and family life sits at the centre of everything. Islam teaches that family values are so important, they should be the foundation of society. In Indonesia, family life is everything. Being a part of family life ensures the development of love and compassion, and provides a lifelong support network.

Indonesians have a powerful sense of responsibility over their family members, especially older ones. In the UK, more than three million employees are juggling employment and caring for elder relatives. In 2014, The Guardian newspaper reported that one in three employers say absenteeism has risen because workers need more time off for caring responsibilities[343]. In a study by Willis Towers Watson[344], the CIPD report that one sixth of employees have caring responsibilities for older family members. Shockingly though, this trend isn't being recognised by employers. A joint report by Westfield Health and the CIPD[345] says that just a third of employers have a policy in place to assist employees with any elder care responsibilities they may have.

In the USA, more than half of caregivers work full-time, and according to the Gallup-Heathways Well-Being Index[346], the demographics of these carers are widespread.

The National Alliance for Caregiving and AARP[347] report that 70 per cent of caregivers suffer work-related difficulties. A massive 69 per cent of employed caregivers are having to take unpaid leave to meet their caregiving responsibilities. Mike Minett, Founder and Managing Director of The Positive Ageing Company (a Mercer brand), thinks employers still aren't taking the issue seriously enough. "Employers need to get their heads around the fact that almost one in nine employees are already working carers and this number will soon be one in six as the ageing population demographic shifts really start to kick in, and eldercare becomes twice the family commitment it ever was". By intervening to help ease the burden of the stress caused by caregiving, employers can benefit too. Minett says "awareness, acknowledgement and simple working carer support measures put in place by an employer can quickly make a real difference to the whole equation, with some positive win-wins to be had for all parties".

As primary caregivers, parents are a child's first source of education, and so home life will have a significant impact on a child's early development. In 2003, the UK launched the Flexible Working Act. This granted parents with children under the age of six, or disabled children, the right to request flexible working. Considering this change, the University of Georgetown[348], Washington D.C published a report into its success. The authors found that three out of four of the employers surveyed reported some or significant improvements in employee relations since offering flexible working. The biggest impact of this change has been seen by working parents.

Cranfield University[349], in association with Working Families, conducted a two-year research project on seven organisations. Their findings showed a direct relationship between flexible working arrangements and an individual employee's performance. The positive impact on the employer, individual employees, and their co-workers was significant. Those employees who were working flexibly were found to be more committed to the organisation, and in some cases, had higher job satisfaction than other employees. The research also pointed to the availability of flexible working being a key competitive strategy for employers against their competitors.

A few years ago, I hosted a roundtable at a conference for people working in Human Resources. The subject up for discussion was employee happiness and how we could improve it. At the start of the session, I asked each member in turn to tell me what the most important thing in their life was. Every single person told me that it was their family and friends. So, the question I posed back at the them to close the session was, "if family and friends are so important to your employees, why isn't everything you do designed around helping them to make the most of those relationships?". We've already seen in this book that making time for relationships outside of work is crucial to our wellbeing, but it can also make us better at our jobs. Spending time with family members can even help us to make healthier food choices[350].

Spending time with our families is something that many employees enjoy doing, and it forms a significant part of their social life.

Researchers at the University of Michigan[351] studied the impact of socialising to see if it can make us smarter. They examined participants' cognitive functioning and the frequency of their social interactions. They found that those participants who more often engaged in socialising displayed higher levels of cognitive performance than others. Socialising can also help employees' health - especially as they get older. Mayo Clinic's National Institute on Ageing[352] carried out a four-year study on 256 older people with an average age of 87. The research showed that socialising with others made participants more than 50 per cent less likely to develop cognitive impairment. The American Association of Retired Persons (AARP) also says that socialising reduces people's risk of developing dementia[353].

In November 2014, then Vice President Joe Biden sent an email to all his staff that soon went viral around the world. In his email, Biden told employees, "I do not expect, nor do I want, any of you to miss or sacrifice important family obligations for work". He went on to say, "I will go as far to say that if I find out that you are working with me while missing important family responsibilities, it will disappoint me greatly". Biden's words rang out around the world, and he was quickly praised by employees and employers alike. However, new research suggests that the average family spends just 34 minutes together each day[354], which is shocking when we consider the implications for not spending enough time with our families.

Teenagers who have infrequent family dinners (fewer than three a week) are more than twice as likely to say that they expect to try drugs in the future, according to a report from The National Center on Addiction and Substance Abuse[355]. Now, that might be an extreme example, but research shows time and time again that spending time together as a family has huge benefits to our wellbeing, especially for our other family members. For example, siblings who spend more time together have higher self-esteem[356]. Teenagers who have developed warm relationships with their parents give higher importance to a 'good personality' than others when looking for ideal traits in a potential partner[357].

It's clear that family responsibilities and spending time with family members can have an impact on an employee's ability to do their work effectively. Employers should be implementing strategies to help employees accommodate their responsibilities and families outside of work. Minett says, "research is already showing that employers who embrace, encourage and even enforce this approach are already enjoying significant benefits. The old models of Monday-to-Friday, 9-to-5 need to be dead and buried. A modern, contemporary workplace should have flexibility, agility, trust and degrees of personal empowerment at its core. By default, this will make the life/work balance of those who are working carers significantly better".

Flexible working is one of the most obvious and popular ways of enabling employees to assist with caregiving and family responsibilities. Creating a work schedule that fits in with the lives of employees can lead to happier and healthier staff. Diane Halpern used data from the US National Study of the Changing Workforce to test the hypothesis that those employees who were given flexible working options reported less stress and higher organisational commitment.

Halpern found that those employers who offered flexible working to allow employees to accommodate the needs of their families are actually financially better off[358]. As we've learnt from BT in the UK, flexible working improved the productivity of call centre operators by 20 per cent[359]. Flexible workers also had 63 per cent less sick leave than office-based employees. Amazingly, BT also found that retention rate after maternity leave was a massive 99 per cent. Proving for them at least, that accommodating the caring responsibilities of a family was a significant benefit to their employees.

23. Conclusion

The Secret is Positivity

Society is evolving at an unprecedented pace, and at times it feels like we are struggling to keep up. Humans continue to evolve, and at an increasing rate, thanks to advances in medicine and larger populations. In just 100 years, our life expectancy has almost doubled, and we're fatter and taller than ever. The pace of change in society has led to generational differences much larger than we've seen before. The Guardian reports that just a 12-year age gap reveals a very different generation. Those born in the 1950s grew up quickly, spent little time in education, and moved straight into work. Those born in the 1970s stretched out their education, lived with their parents for longer, and extended their youth into their twenties. Fast forward to the 2000s, and the youngest workers are much more likely to be living at home while progressing their careers.

House prices have grown far higher than wages since 1980, and the group that these changes have affected the most are younger employees. There are fewer people aged 16 to 34 in 2017 who own their own home than there has ever been in the last 20 years[360]. This has created a new workforce who are less motivated by earning money to pay a mortgage, and are struggling financially more than any other generation in almost 40 years. They also have less job security than perhaps any other age group in recent memory.

As we learned at the start of this book, the situation is challenging for employers too. Global productivity is on the decline and the knock-on effects this has on our economy is huge. Poor productivity slows down our economic growth. Could we improve global productivity by encouraging employers to invest more in their employees? The most progressive organisations have already realised this is true, and you'll see from some of the case studies in this book, the investment isn't about spending more money on employees. Steven Moore and his co-author Michael Mankins, found that the efforts companies make to improve life for their employees really does pay off. In their book, Time, Talent and Energy, Moore and Mankins found that the top 25 per cent of companies they studied, unlocked 40 per cent more productivity when they invested in their employees.

Organisations need to understand that workplace evolution is rapid too. The pace and the dominance of technology is bringing with it new challenges we had never considered just 10 years ago. This prevalence of technology at work is leading to an increasing demand for more human-orientated skills, and a more 'human' Human Resources. The traditional ways of working, (usually enshrined in law) are no longer fit for purpose, and HR is no longer a process-orientated role. It's less about policy and procedure, and more about coaching and guidance. The psychological demand on employees has never been greater and creating a new workplace for a new world is imperative.

From taking regular breaks to finding our purpose, diverse cultures from around the world can teach us about how we can design the workplace to best fit our new, more human-centric needs. However, the biggest barrier to changing our workplace has less to do with what we do, and more to do with how we think about it. A 2010 study found that positive thinking was the key to happiness[361]. How we see our world every day is what will affect our happiness, so the workplace will have an enormous impact on this[362].

Some of the cultural practices in this book are just an analogy for what psychology says we humans need. When we look at the 10 essential metrics employees need from their working lives, we'll recognise most of them. In 2016, Officevibe started a long-term, real-time study into what employees needed from their work in order to be happy and productive[363]. More than 50,000 employees from 100,000 different organisations around the world gave their views. One of the top 10 things employees said they needed was happiness. Twenty-three per cent of global employees say they leave work feeling drained, run down, exhausted and unhappy.

To understand how the employer/employee relationship has changed over the years, we can turn to LinkedIn. Oleg Vishnepolsky, CTO at Daily Mail Online and Metro.co.uk collated LinkedIn's most liked and shared articles of time[364]. There was a common theme among those posts that had been shared more than 100,000 times: the employee is in charge.

Posts included many inspirational quotes including Sir Richard Branson's famous quote, "clients do not come first. Employees come first", as well as Peter Drucker's, "never push loyal people to the point where they don't give a damn". The number one most liked article of all time (liked more than 250,000 times) was one about leaving the office on time. The article reminded us that we are not machines and that our families and friends are the most important things in our lives. On a work-related social networking site, the most liked article discusses how work should not be everything to us. I think that's quite telling.

To really understand what an employee wants, we just need to look at the kinds of organisations they want to work for. In 2017, Morning Consult surveyed almost 250,000 Americans to see what companies they most admired, and who they wanted to work for[365]. The top six were Google, Tesla, Amazon, Disney, Microsoft and Apple. All these companies have appeared in this book as examples of good employers whose working practices have been praised around the world. These are the companies that are most visible to potential employees as an employer that will invest in, and take care of them. These progressive organisations are paving the way for the future of work, and are doing so by putting the employee and their needs at the centre of their business. Their influence is ensuring that even the most archaic employer changes their attitude to their employees.

As attention to the employee experience grows, many organisations are struggling to know what they need to do for an increasingly demanding and diverse workforce. Encouraging happiness, productivity, and good culture in the workplace isn't an easy thing to do at all, and getting it right for everyone is the holy grail. Creating a positive atmosphere in the workplace is such a tricky thing to achieve because we have a built in negative bias. Negativity has a bigger impact on our brains than positivity has, so we must work hard to be positive. However, there are some very compelling bits of research that are starting to tell us what the secret to the perfect employee experience might be. It lies in how employees feel about themselves.

The IBM Smarter Workforce Institute and Globoforce's Work Human Research Institute recently conducted one of the largest studies of its kind to find out what the secret to a great employee experience was[366]. The study involved more than 23,000 employees from 45 different countries to give an entire world view. The research shows what most of us already know when thinking about what employees need from work. Feeling part of a team, understanding our purpose, a sense of accomplishment and a sense of excitement at work are all characteristics of high-performing employees. These are the features that contribute to our Ikigai and give us a sense of belonging. Having a sense of belonging (especially at work) has become critical to our mental health. So important is it that the World Health Organisation cite it as a core component of mental health and wellbeing[367].

There was one consistent theme in IBM and Globoforce's study; employees worked harder and committed more when there were more positive experiences at work. The more positivity an employer brings to the workplace, the more 'over and above' effort employees give. The common theme in all the lessons we've learnt, from Africa to Bhutan, and France to China, is that they are all positive. Every lesson is built around improving the experience of the employee.

Whether it's accommodating their lives outside of work, encouraging them to find their own purpose, improving working practices, or encouraging social interactions, every lesson is designed to create a positive experience - and that is the real lesson.

When employees have meaningful work, relationships, and experiences at work, they are more likely to bond with each other as well as the organisation and its values. Almost 90 per cent of employees say they want their happiness to be measured as part of their employment[368]. Happiness at work is a relatively new theme. For a long time, employees weren't rewarded for a job well done, they were simply fired if they didn't work hard enough; the result of a system of punishment instilled in many generations from when they were at school. However, at some point over the last 50 years; the threat of a stick gave way to the lure of a carrot.

A recent study conducted at an American state hospital may help us understand why punishment no longer works[369].

Employees weren't washing their hands as much as they should have been and despite the frequent management objections and warning signs about the spread of diseases, nothing improved. For this hospital study, employees weren't punished for not washing their hands, but instead congratulated when they did. Every time an employee washed their hands, an electronic board displayed positive messages and increased that employee's 'scores'. The volume of employees now washing their hands increased to almost 90 per cent within just a few weeks. It wasn't the fear of reprisal that motivated these employees to comply with the hand washing rules, it was the lure of a positive message. Similar psychological studies have found that we are much more susceptible and motivated by positive messages than negative ones.

Disney CEO Robert Iger (tipped to be running as a Democrat in the 2020 US election), thinks there is no room to be anything but positive when it comes to running a business[370]. Iger told CNBC, "no-one wants to follow a pessimist… You can be sceptical, you can be realistic, but you can't be cynical"[371]. Iger thinks employees look for positivity at work and when they do, they look to their leaders. He adds, "if your boss is Eeyore, do you want to work with someone like that? Oh, bother". We've already seen in this book how Disney treats its employees in a very progressive way and part of that has been influenced by Iger. Since taking the helm Iger bought Pixar, turned ESPN into a media giant and acquired Marvel and Lucasfilm. He's achieved wonderful things and has done it with the support and commitment of his employees.

Surrounding ourselves with positivity is one of the secrets to a happy life. Developing a positive mental attitude, banishing negative thoughts and surrounding ourselves with positive people is every psychologist's advice to leading a happier and healthier life. Negative emotions and experiences program our brains to react in a certain way. For example, when negativity produces fear, our flight instincts kick in. Therefore, it is important that we try to improve our daily exposure to positivity. In a landmark study, Barbara Fredrickson looked at how people's daily experiences of positivity compound over time[372]. The study revealed the more daily positivity a person experiences, the healthier they were.

Decreased illness and depression, increased social support, and increased life satisfaction were all benefits of positivity. Fredrickson also found that positivity broadens our sense of possibilities and opens our minds to new experiences. This helps employees develop new skills.

Psychologists often refer to something called an 'upward spiral' that's common in people who consider themselves positive. These people are happy, able to develop new skills, and this leads to success. Positive, happy people focus on being happy first, and success follows. Employers should be doing the same. If employers create an environment that encourages happiness and positivity, the results will soon follow.

Nick Gianoulis, Founder and 'Godfather of Fun' at The Fun Dept. and co-author of Playing It Forward, says that positivity should include employees having more fun at work. Gianoulis told me, "the right kind of fun starts with what is actually fun for the employees, not something that HR sees on a team building company's website. Or worse yet, what the boss thinks is fun is typically much different than what employees view as fun". When I interviewed Gianoulis, he told me all about 'The Shared Experience'. The Shared Experience is a straightforward process that helps identify the common themes for fun in any organisation.

Gianoulis says, "by asking employees what is fun for them and then building all-inclusive and non-threatening simple activities, you set yourself up for success. He adds, "schedule brief activities (15-30 min) once per month on company time. By treating fun as a process instead of some event, organisations can see measurable results within 6 months to a year". Fun has a positive effect on our motivation levels and can determine how much we learn and retain[373]. Positivity and fun at work isn't about allowing employees time to mess around, its about creating a culture that people want to spend time in.

Nick Court, Founder and CEO of Cloud9 People thinks it's not just about increasing the positive messages, but removing the points of frustration and unhappiness. Court says, "instead, measure the things that are detrimental to the overall employee experience while at work.

Ensure that there is nothing in work that would contribute to making an employee less satisfied, less engaged or less motivated (this is why our survey measures inputs, not outputs)". Court says that employers have limited ability to change an employee's home life, but that they can change their work life for the better.

Court sees this delicate balance as an equation:

Bad Work Life + Good Home Life
= Resilient Employee Can Cope
Good Work Life + Bad Home Life
= Resilient Employee Can Cope
Bad Work Life + Bad Home Life
= Employee Will Not Cope

Court has tapped into how modern employees struggle to manage both work lives and home lives, especially as the two are now so often intertwined. Employers and employees need to be doing what they can to ease the burden of everyday living for employees. I believe that is the key to building the best outcomes at work. How and where employees work will have a significant impact on the work they produce.

Almost half of employees believe their current working environment does not positively impact their happiness[374] and that's a big problem.

In their research, psychologists Myeong-Gu Seo, Lisa Feldman and Jean Bartunek revealed that there is a direct connection between an employee's emotional experience at work and how motivated they generally were[375].

For us to thrive, research reveals we need an experience ratio of three to one[376]. This means for every negative experience we have, we need three positive experiences. To counter balance the negativity associated with old technology, archaic processes or disruptive work environments, employers have never had to work harder to create more positivity at work. It's almost like two steps forward and one step back. However, if employers don't get that magic ratio, their employees are at increased risk of unhappiness, stress and burnout. Stress is killing our workforces, literally. It is estimated that more than 80 per cent of doctor visits are linked to stress[377].

It's America's number-one health problem. In the UK, work causes mental health issues in 60 per cent of the workforce[378]. Alarmingly, 15 per cent of employees are afraid to tell their employers about mental health issues for fear of negative reprisals[379]. This cannot continue. It's already sweeping across every industry.

Employers should be creating a more supportive and positive work culture that accommodates employees' lives outside of work as a minimum. From enabling remote/home working to encouraging social interactions and offering support, looking after the happiness and wellbeing of employees makes financial sense.

The American Psychological Association believes that more than $500 billion a year is being lost from the US economy due to stress caused at work[380]. High pressure work cultures are spending nearly 50 per cent more than others on health care expenses[381]. Organisations that create and maintain positive work environments produce better results than those that don't. But this positivity cannot be faked – employees will remember how employers made them feel for a long time[382].

When we allow employees to open up and be themselves at work, they have a better experience. Encouraging a climate of authenticity improves the workplace, and even lessens the individual's chances of stress and burnout[383]. Positive work cultures need to be built on a genuine care for the wellbeing of employees. As we've seen, giving trust and showing compassion yield the best results for all involved.

A common theme throughout all the cultural practices and research in this book has been flexibility. The rise of the gig economy has proven that employees are keen to explore innovative ways of working that can fit in with their busy social and personal lives. More than a third of 16 to 30-year-olds are currently working in the UK gig economy, and that number is expected to rise rapidly[384].

The UK is also seeing a sizeable increase in the number of self-employed workers too[385]. Around 15 per cent of all of those working in the UK are now self-employed.

The flexibility to work in a way that suits the individual at a location that works best for them is now one of the strongest pulls to a job. When we decorate our homes and buy our sofas, we do it in a way that makes us comfortable. We surround ourselves with items and photographs that make us happy. We actively create a safe environment. Allowing employees to work from their own 'safe place' is beneficial to the employee/employer relationship. In addition, it also builds unique levels of trust. Telling an employee that "I trust you and I'm empowering you to make the right decision" sits at the start of flexible working or results-orientated strategies. To get the best out of employees, organisations need to understand what is holding them back.

In his book The Inner Game of Work, author Tim Gallwey introduces an equation on performance:

$$\mathbf{P=p-i}$$

$$\text{Performance} = \text{potential - interference}$$

Our performance is equal to what we are capable of only when we remove obstacles (interferences). Just like Court told me, it's not just the increase in positivity, but the decrease in negativity. The negative interference that is impeding performance could be anything from the noise in the office, a micro-managing leader, a tired head or frustrating technology. Employers should be exploring ways to remove areas of inference as part of improving their positivity.

Allowing employees to avoid the morning commute, to work at home a few days of the week, or to take a longer lunch break, could make all the difference to helping them realise their true potential.

Employers have focused a lot on trying to make employees happy at work by offering perks. The problem with perks is that people tend to adapt to things that happen regularly. Giving frequent small positive experiences work, but only when the focus is also on the things that employees really want and things that go much deeper than a free coffee. One of the keys to improving employee happiness is making sure staff have new, enjoyable experiences whenever they can. Even more so than material or monetary rewards, people want to enjoy themselves, and the impact of a positive life experience can last for a long time.

Reminding employees of the positive experiences you have been able to facilitate, and encouraging reflection on them, ensures employees practice gratitude[386] - something research says increases our health and happiness[387]. The surprising thing about giving employees new, fun experiences is they benefit from looking forward to them too. As we've seen with our annual vacation, the anticipation we get in the build-up to something can make us happier than doing the thing itself. For employers, if you do this, you get two bites of the cherry. You get to give your employees a positive experience twice; once by telling them about the reward and allowing them to look forward to it, and then again when you deliver the reward.

Neuroscience tells us that people make decisions using emotion, not logic. One of the world's leading neuroscientists Antonio Damasio examined one of his patients in a world-famous study[388]. In assessing the damage to his patient's front lobe as the result of a tumour, Damasio found that his patient had become incapable of making decisions. He found that this highly intelligent, once successful businessman was suffering with making even the smallest decisions. This examination led to the idea that emotion assists our reasoning processes. It's also now widely believed that our motivation is driven by how we feel, not how we think. Armed with that knowledge, business leaders and HR teams must realise that the emotive side of work is now what drives employees to succeed. As we saw from Lutgen-Sandvik et al, an employee's positive experiences at work are driven by emotive aspects like contributing to organisational success, building relationships with colleagues, being trusted, and being recognised for a job well done[389].

The Employee Experience Index by IBM Smarter Workforce, shows that a positive employee experience is linked to better performance. Those employers with high employee experience index scores are more likely to report higher levels of employee performance. They also found that the more positivity that could be found in an employee's experience, the more discretionary effort employees make. This discretionary effort is more than twice as likely to occur when the employee experience is positive. Positive experiences, unsurprisingly, also encourage lower turnover rates in an organisation.

It is clear that positive experiences are the mechanisms of change and the foundation of a great employee experience. The more positive experiences an employer can facilitate and the less negative hassles their employees encounter, the happier, healthier, and more productive employees will be. A study published in the Journal of Research in Personality looked at two groups of students to see how positivity impacted their lives[390]. In one group, students were asked to write about a very positive experience every day, for three days in a row. The second group were asked to write about a control topic. After three months, the results were analysed along with any changes in the students' lives. Amazingly, those students who focussed each day on a positive experience reported fewer visits to health centres, improved mood and even fewer illnesses.

For employers to create the right positive culture at work, there will be some employees they'll just need to get rid of. It sounds harsh, but those disengaged, negative employees that you are unable to turn around are affecting your business like a silent virus. In her book, Inspirational Gamechangers, author Rita Clifton says, "there are people who behave like radiators and there are people who behave like drains". If your organisation has disengaged, negative employees, they are affecting the employee experience of your other, more engaged employees. Glassdoor says that people will share their good experiences with three people, but their bad ones with 10 or more[391]. Disengaged employees will spread their negative brand to other employees quickly. Recruiting the right personalities and removing the wrong ones must form part of any employer's cultural strategy.

In an interview with HR Grapevine, Lisa Robbins, HR Director at Starbucks says, "at Starbucks, we hire on attitude rather than experience or qualifications"[392]. Robbins believes that being an effective team player, having excellent communication skills and great customer service, are among the most important and desirable traits. Robbins also sees being a caring person as a personality trait Starbucks wants from its employees.

Our final country lesson comes from Africa, quoted in the book, We are the Ones we Have Been Waiting for: Inner Light in a Time of Darkness, by Alice Walker. Walker tells us of a ritual of an African tribe called the Babemba. In this South African tribe, when a person is irresponsible or makes a mistake, they are taken to the centre of the village. Immediately, all work stops, and every villager is encouraged to form a circle around this person. Each villager then takes it in turns to talk to the person who made a mistake and share their thoughts. However, they don't berate or belittle the accused.

They don't even scold them. Each villager is encouraged to recall all the good things and positive memories they have about this person. All that person's positive traits and actions are regaled, and their strengths and kindnesses remembered. This ceremony often lasts for many days and at the end, the circle is broken, and the villagers celebrate. The person is welcomed back into the tribe and life goes on. The tribe believes in positivity, compassion and kindness. Do you think the Babemba tribe have got the right idea?

Psychologists who have researched how humans forgive have found that in criminals, our current strategies are counterproductive, and the reduction in re-offending is linked to how we forgive. In one peer review, psychologists reported that we have an 'evolutionarily endowed capacity' to forgive people[393]. I use this as an extreme example, but it shows how promoting the positive aspects of employees can make things better for everyone at work. The Scientific American reports that the secret to a happy romantic relationship is to accentuate the positive as much as you can[394]. Maybe it's time we started doing the same with our work relationship?

A study published by the Harvard Medical School thinks employee appreciation is the secret to a positive employee experience. The study by the Wharton Medical School at the University of Pennsylvania studied university fund raisers[395]. These students were made to telephone university alumni to try and get donations. The students were split into two groups; one group made their calls the usual way, but the other group received a positive talk from their fundraising director who told them how grateful she was for their efforts. Subsequently, the employees who received the pep talk made 50 per cent more fundraising calls than the other group. Showing gratitude is core to mindfulness and practicing it openly will soon be commonplace at work.

Every employee has an experience at work and it's the employer's responsibility to remove as much negativity from this experience as possible. A great employee experience can only be achieved with positivity. The removal of negative emotions from the workplace is the only way you can ensure employees perform at their best. A football coach doesn't want his star player to be upset or distracted, and a film director doesn't want his lead actress to be worried. As employers can't remove all negativity at work alone, your future employees will play a part in helping you shape this positive culture.

Recruiting employees that fit the culture you want to promote will be one of the key strategies of HR in the next few years. The skills will become far less important than the personality. As artificial intelligence and automation continue to dominate the workplace, those employees with empathy, creativity and a positive attitude will become the most desirable candidates. Starbucks realised this long before other employers have.

In October 2017, the London newspaper, City AM published the results of Glassdoor's top UK companies by workplace culture[396]. They also published the management attitude and ethos of the culture of those organisations. The UK's top employer was Northern Gas and Power who feel that "nothing is more important here than managerial behaviour".

Third on the list was Equal Experts whose culture is defined as; "When people enjoy what they are doing, they create better work, day in, day out". Homeserve UK (who came in at sixth on the list) say, "if you put your people first, they will look after your customers and the rest will take care of itself".

Finally, the ninth best UK company for culture was Auto Trader, who say, "an important part of our culture is to address negative behaviour in a timely manner, so all managers take responsibility for this". Other organisations in the top 10 included Facebook, Skyscanner and Badoo. These employers couldn't be more different in the services or products they sell, but one thing unites them all – the way they treat and think about their employees. Every single organisation in the top 20 admits to putting employees' needs at the centre of their organisation.

The significant changes being brought about by some of the most progressive organisations around the world is having a profound impact. Ben Whitter, 'Mr Employee Experience', and founder, World Employee Experience Institute (WEEI) says, "what we are seeing around the world is nothing short of a global awakening. Organisations worldwide are waking up to the fact that they really do need to thoughtfully consider and place the employee experience at the very top of the business agenda. Why? Because it makes absolute business sense to do so".

Whitter adds, “the very top measure of employee experience is business results, and the businesses getting ahead of their competitors understand and invest in the experience of work on a scale that most can’t comprehend. They know and embrace this not-so-secret recipe to organisational success”. At the end of our interview, Whitter really summed up what the future of the workplace is: “Business is all about the quality of the experience for both customers and employees. This is great news for everyone - enjoy the experience”.

The employee must sit at the centre of any company. Employees are commonly referred to as “an organisation’s best resource” – but they aren’t resources at all. Employees are people. Employers now have a requirement to treat employees as humans and they must be treated with humanity. The American Psychological Association believes this is so important that they are now actively honouring those organisations who foster a psychologically healthy workplace[397].

More than eight out of 10 employees working at each of the organisations that have been honoured, value the following six workplace traits and attitudes that make them feel mentally healthy and appreciated[398]:

- Values the involvement of employees
- Enables a work/life balance
- Offers training and development
- Recognises the work of employees
- Supports a healthy lifestyle
- Helps them manage stress

Ways to implement the above practices can be found throughout this book. Home/flexible working, forest bathing, regular breaks, recognition – all these things drive the employee to work in a way that is positive, enjoyable and meaningful. I think that's the secret to creating the best employee experience, wherever you are in the world.

Enjoy discovering your own… **World of Good.**

REFERENCES

[1] **The Huffington Post:**

http://www.huffingtonpost.com/robert-leahy-phd/unemployment-health_b_2616430.html

[2] **The Lancet:**

http://www.thelancet.com/journals/lancet/article/PIIS0140-6736(96)03291-6/abstract

[3] **Revise Sociology:**

https://revisesociology.com/2016/08/16/percentage-life-work/

[4] **UK Business Insider:**

http://uk.businessinsider.com/how-the-world-has-changed-in-100-years-2015-12

[5] **BT:**

https://www2.bt.com/static/i/media/pdf/flex_working_wp_07.pdf

6 **Quartz Media:**

https://qz.com/302264/the-best-places-in-the-world-to-work-in-7-charts/

7 **Sky News:**

https://news-sky-com.cdn.ampproject.org/c/news.sky.com/story/amp/who-are-the-uks-most-unhappiest-workers-11053588

[8] **AON:**

http://img04.en25.com/Web/AonMcLagan/%7B0d276379-e0c7-43da-a58d-da6eb92bba87%7D_Talent_2021.pdf

9 **Forbes:**

https://www-forbes-com.cdn.ampproject.org/c/s/www.forbes.com/sites/cameronkeng/2014/06/22/employees-that-stay-in-companies-longer-than-2-years-get-paid-50-less/amp/

10 **USA Today:**

https://www.usatoday.com/story/money/personalfinance/2013/09/18/how-much-of-a-pay-raise-can-you-expect-in-2014/2832791/

11 **PwC:**

https://www.pwc.com/gx/en/managing-tomorrows-people/future-of-work/assets/reshaping-the-workplace.pdf

12 **The Telegraph:**
http://www.telegraph.co.uk/finance/jobs/10559605/Half-of-young-workers-ready-for-career-switch.html
13 **GQ Magazine:**
http://www.gq-magazine.co.uk/article/battling-burnout-overworking-stress-depression
14 **Personnel Psychology:**
http://hermanaguinis.com/PPsych2014.pdf
15 **Deloitte:**
https://www2.deloitte.com/content/dam/Deloitte/global/Documents/HumanCapital/hc-2017-global-human-capital-trends-gx.pdf
[16] **IBM Smarter Workforce Institute:**
http://www.globoforce.com/wp-content/uploads/2016/10/The_Employee_Experience_Index.pdf
17 **National Centre for Biotechnology Information:**
https://www.ncbi.nlm.nih.gov/pmc/articles/PMC1351035/
18 **Cognition:**
Atsunori Ariga, Alejandro Lleras. Brief and rare mental 'breaks' keep you focused: Deactivation and reactivation of task goals preempt vigilance decrements. Cognition, 2011; DOI: 10.1016/j.cognition.2010.12.007
19 **Science Direct:**
http://www.sciencedirect.com/science/article/pii/S074959781630108X
[20] **Harvard Gazette:**
https://news.harvard.edu/gazette/story/2010/11/wandering-mind-not-a-happy-mind/
[21] **Unum:**
http://www.unum.co.uk/hr/the-future-workplace
[22] **Proceedings of the National Academy of Sciences:**
Kalina Christoff, Alan M. Gordon, Jonathan Smallwood, Rachelle Smith, and Jonathan W. Schooler. Experience sampling during fMRI reveals default network and executive system contributions to mind wandering. Proceedings of the National Academy of Sciences, 2009; DOI: 10.1073/pnas.0900234106

[23] **BMC Public Health:**

https://bmcpublichealth.biomedcentral.com/articles/10.1186/1471-2458-12-253

[24] **Academy of Management:**

http://m.amp.aom.org/content/20/2/58.short

[25] **BrightHR:**

https://pages.brighthr.com/itpaystoplay-v3.html

[26] **The Walt Disney Company:**

https://thewaltdisneycompany.com/philanthropy/

[27] **LifeHacker:**

http://lifehacker.com/52-minute-work-17-minute-break-is-the-ideal-productivi-1616541102

[28] **Science Direct:**

http://www.sciencedirect.com/science/article/pii/S074959781630108X

[29] **Public Library of Science:**

Nittono H, Fukushima M, Yano A, Moriya H (2012) The Power of Kawaii: Viewing Cute Images Promotes a Careful Behavior and Narrows Attentional Focus. PLoS ONE 7(9): e46362. doi:10.1371/journal.pone.0046362

[30] **University of Michigan:**

https://record.umich.edu/articles/do-you-have-passion-your-job-if-not-its-attainable

[31] **Sage Journals:**

Finding a Fit or Developing It. Implicit Theories About Achieving Passion for Work. Patricia Chen, Phoebe C. Ellsworth, Norbert Schwarz. First Published July 31, 2015 research-article

[32] **Fast Company:**

https://www.fastcompany.com/3069200/heres-what-faceb%E2%80%A6ployee-happiness

[33] **Physiology & Behavior:** Testosterone changes during vicarious experiences of winning and losing among fans at sporting events'. Paul C Bernhardt*, James M Dabbs Jr, Julie A Fielden, Candice D Lutter University of Utah, Dept. of Educational Psychology, MBH 327, Salt Lake City, USA. Georgia State University, Dept. of Psychology, Atlanta. Physiology & Behavior. Vol 65, 1, August 1998, Pages 59–62

[34] **Business Insider:**

http://uk.businessinsider.com/why-millennials-wont-work-in-oil-2017-7?r=US&IR=T

[35] **HR Magazine:**

http://www.hrmagazine.co.uk/article-details/increase-number-of-older-workers-by-12-employers-told

[36] **US News:**

https://www.usnews.com/news/articles/2015-12-24/older-workers-to-dominate-labor-market-by-2024)

[37] **Institute for Employment Studies:**

Fulfilling Work: What do older workers value about work and why? Rosa Marvell and Annette Cox. Centre for Better Ageing/Institute for employment studies, Feb 2017.

[38] **PayScale:**

http://www.payscale.com/data-packages/top-tech-companies-compared

[39] **Science Daily:**

https://www.sciencedaily.com/releases/2016/02/160211184959.htm

[40] **University of Notre Dame:**

Encouraging Motivation to Benefit Others Can Lead to More Effective Teams. Article ID: 643176. Released 13th November, 2015.

[41] **Fast Company:**

https://www.fastcompany.com/3055415/apples-angela-ahrendts-on-what-it-takes-to-make-change-inside-a-successful-business

[42] **UK Business Insider:**

http://uk.businessinsider.com/best-things-about-working-at-apple-2016-1/#employees-love-the-discounts-they-get-on-apple-products-3

[43] **Gallup:**

http://www.gallup.com/businessjournal/195491/few-employees-believe-company-values.aspx

[44] **Marginalia Online:**

http://www.marginalia.online/faking-company-values-damages-your-career/

[45] **BioMed Central:**
https://sleep.biomedcentral.com/articles/10.1186/s41606-017-0015-6
[46] **Business Culture:**
http://businessculture.org/southern-europe/business-culture-in-italy/work-life-balance-in-italy/
[47] **PR Newswire:**
http://www.prnewswire.com/news-releases/birra-moretti-encourages-americans-to-enjoy-lunch-like-italians-123989634.html
[48] **The National Charity Partnership:**
A collaboration between Diabetes UK, the British Heart Foundation (BHF) and Tesco: http://tescocharitypartnership.org.uk/
[49] **Total Jobs:**
https://www.totaljobs.com/insidejob/price-lunch-breaks-research/
[50] **Behaviour Research and Therapy:**
Crane C et al, "The effects of amount of home meditation practice in Mindfulness Based Cognitive Therapy on hazard of relapse to depression in the Staying Well after Depression Trial", Behaviour Research and Therapy, 2014
[51] **Pennsylvania State University:**
What Are the Benefits of Mindfulness? A Practice Review of Psychotherapy-Related Research Daphne M. Davis and Jeffrey A. Hayes, Pennsylvania State University.
[52] **Baylor:**
https://www.baylor.edu/mediacommunications/news.php?action=story&story=159785
[53] **Berkeley University of California:**
http://thriving.berkeley.edu/sites/default/files/Embracing%20Work%20Breaks%20(Eschleman%20Lecture).pdf
[54] **Berkeley University of California:**
http://thriving.berkeley.edu/sites/default/files/Embracing%20Work%20Breaks%20(Eschleman%20Lecture).pdf
[55] **Canadian Association of Municipal Administrators**:
http://www.camacampaign.ca/6-2016_-_Why_a_Lunch_Break_Will_Increase_Productivity_in_Your_Organization.pdf

[56] **The Muse:**

https://www.themuse.com/advice/the-rule-of-52-and-17-its-random-but-it-ups-your-productivity

[57] **American Society for Clinical Nutrition:**

Dietary protein, carbohydrate, and fat enhance memory performance in the healthy elderly1,2,3. Randall J Kaplan, Carol E Greenwood, Gordon Winocur, and Thomas MS Wolever, 2001. American Society for Clinical Nutrition.

[58] **Live Science:**

https://www.livescience.com/3186-brain-food-eat-smart.html

[59] **National Center for Biomedical Information:**

https://www.ncbi.nlm.nih.gov/pubmed?Db=pubmed&Cmd=ShowDetailView&TermToSearch=17998028&ordinalpos=1&itool=EntrezSystem2.PEntrez.Pubmed.Pubmed_ResultsPanel.Pubmed_RVDocSum

[60] **The Telegraph:**

http://www.telegraph.co.uk/finance/jobs/11326076/British-workers-are-skipping-lunch-and-thats-hurting-productivity.html

[61] **The New York Times:**

https://www.nytimes.com/2017/04/18/opinion/youre-too-busy-you-need-a-shultz-hour.html?_r=0

[62] **Hansgrohe:**

http://www1.hansgrohe.com/assets/at--de/1404_Hansgrohe_Select_ConsumerSurvey_EN.pdf

[63] **Psychological Science:**

http://www.psychologicalscience.org/news/releases/more-than-just-zoning-out-psychological-science-examines-the-cognitive-processes-underlying-mind-wandering.html#.WQxrKYjytEY

[64] **Nature:**

https://www.nature.com/articles/srep38866

[65] **Annuls of Internal Medicine:**

http://annals.org/aim/article/2653704/patterns-sedentary-behavior-mortality-u-s-middle-aged-older-adults

[66] **Johnson and Johnson Human Performance Institute:**

http://corporateathleteedge.com/issue/jul_aug12

[67] **Public Library of Science:**

http://journals.plos.org/plosone/article?id=10.1371/journal.pone.0070314

[68] **Proceedings of the National Academy of Science of the United States of America:**

Experience sampling during fMRI reveals default network and executive system contributions to mind wandering. Kalina Christoff, Alan M. Gordon, Jonathan Smallwood, Rachelle Smith[a] and Jonathan W. Schooler. Edited by Michael I. Posner, University of Oregon, Eugene, OR, and approved March 27, 2009.

[69] **Gallup:**

http://www.gallup.com/reports/199961/state-american-workplace-report-2017.aspx

[70] **Spiegel:**

http://www.spiegel.de/international/europe/interview-with-french-president-emmanuel-macron-a-1172745.html

[71] **Gallup:**

http://news.gallup.com/businessjournal/106912/turning-around-your-turnover-problem.aspx

[72] **The Independent:**

https://inews.co.uk/essentials/news/uk/sports-direct-summons-workers-choose-sad-emoji-see-managers/

[73] **INC.com:**

https://www.inc.com/justin-bariso/ubers-new-ceo-just-sent-an-amazing-email-to-employees-taught-a-major-lesson-in-emotional-intelligence.html

[74] **The Wall Street Journal:**

https://www-wsj-com.cdn.ampproject.org/c/s/www.wsj.com/amp/articles/after-uber-boards-wake-up-to-company-culture-1507046401

[75] **Fortune:**

http://fortune.com/2015/03/05/best-companies-greatest-tool-is-culture/

[76] **Great Place to Work:**

https://www.greatplacetowork.com/list-calendar/small-medium-workplaces

[77] **Fortune:**

http://fortune.com/2017/01/05/a-new-study-shows-that-nice-guys-finish-with-higher-revenue/

[78] **Sage Journals:**

http://journals.sagepub.com/doi/pdf/10.1177/1038411109355374

[79] **Gallup:**

http://www.gallup.com/businessjournal/182228/managers-engaged-jobs.aspx

[80] **ACAS:**

http://www.acas.org.uk/index.aspx?articleid=2701

[81] **News.Au**:

http://www.news.com.au/finance/work/leaders/why-pepsico-ceo-asks-his-team-to-leave-loudly/news-story/5467b3ffff387c3a5dd79ac3a245c868

[82] **Emerald Insight:**

http://www.emeraldinsight.com/doi/abs/10.1108/01437731011043348?journalCode=lodj

[83] **Recruit Loop:**

http://recruitloop.com/blog/can-you-justify-having-a-flexible-workforce/

[84] **Annual Reviews:**

http://www.annualreviews.org/doi/full/10.1146/annurev-orgpsych-031413-091221

[85] **Electrek:**

https://electrek.co/2017/06/02/elon-musk-tesla-injury-factory/

[86] **The Independent:**

http://www.independent.co.uk/news/world/europe/six-hour-working-day-sweden-boosts-productivity-and-makes-people-happier-a7023741.html

[87] **Bloomberg:**

https://www.bloomberg.com/news/articles/2017-04-17/how-the-six-hour-workday-actually-saves-money

[88] **Institute for the Study of Labor:**

The Productivity of Working Hours, John Pencavel. Institute for the Study of Labor. April 2014. IZA DP No. 8129

[89] **Nordic Social Statistical Committee:**

Nordic Social Statistical Committee Copenhagen 2015 ISBN 978-87-90248-67-3

[90] **YouGov:**
https://d25d2506sfb94s.cloudfront.net/cumulus_uploads/document/bwlqrh49mv/InternalResults_151012_WorkHours_Website.pdf
[91] **Monthly Labor Review:**
https://www.bls.gov/opub/mlr/2007/04/art2full.pdf
[92] **Oxford Academic:**
https://academic.oup.com/aje/article/169/5/596/143020/Long-Working-Hours-and-Cognitive-FunctionThe
[93] **The Telegraph:**
http://www.telegraph.co.uk/news/2017/10/23/20-minute-increase-commute-time-bad-taking-pay-cut-study-finds/
[94] **ACAS:**
http://www.acas.org.uk/media/pdf/f/2/Home-is-where-the-work-is-a-new-study-of-homeworking-in-Acas_and-beyond.pdf
[95] **Pew Research Centre:**
http://www.pewsocialtrends.org/2013/01/30/the-sandwich-generation/
[96]**Aging Care:**
https://www.agingcare.com/Articles/state-of-caregiving-2015-report-177710.htm
[97] **Senate Intelligence Committee:**
Senate Intelligence Committee report on the CIA's "enhanced interrogation techniques
[98] **RAND:**
Why sleep matters — the economic costs of insufficient sleep: A cross-country comparative analysis. by Marco Hafner, Martin Stepanek, Jirka Taylor, Wendy M. Troxel, Christian Van Stolk. RAND Corporation 2016
[99] **Occupational and Environmental Medicine:**
Moderate sleep deprivation produces impairments in cognitive and motor performance equivalent to legally prescribed levels of alcohol intoxication – Occupational and Environmental Medicine, Vol. 57, Issue 10. A M Williamsona, Anne-Marie Feyerb

[100] **Association for Psychological Science:**
Sleepy Punishers Are Harsh Punishers. Daylight Saving Time and Legal Sentences Kyoungmin Cho, Christopher M. Barnes, Cristiano L. Guanara, First Published December 13, 2016 research-article
[101] **Journal of Experimental Psychology:**
The impact of sleep deprivation on decision making: a review. Journal of Experimental Psychology: Applied. 2000 Volo. 6, No 3. 236-249. Yvonne Harrison, James A Horne, Loughborough University
[102] **US Chamber Foundation:**
https://www.uschamberfoundation.org/enterprisingstates/assets/files/Executive-Summary-OL.pdf
[103] **National Center for Biomedical Information:**
https://www.ncbi.nlm.nih.gov/pubmed/10329298
[104] **CNBC:**
Sleep Health: A shared responsibility, CNBC Innovation Cities 2014
[105] **The Daily Mail:**
http://www.dailymail.co.uk/sciencetech/article-4256198/Interactive-map-reveals-people-struggling-sleep.html#ixzz4fD1LnbI0
[106] **World Crunch:**
https://www.worldcrunch.com/culture-society/buenos-aires-wakes-up-to-the-importance-of-new-age-siestas
[107] **Personality and Individual Differences:**
Napping to modulate frustration and impulsivity: A pilot study. Jennifer R. Goldschmied, Philip Cheng, Kathryn Kemp, Lauren Caccamo, Julia Roberts, Patricia J. Deldin. Personality and Individual Differences. Volume 86, November 2015, Pages 164–167
[108] **Society for Human Resource Management:**
https://www.shrm.org/ResourcesAndTools/hr-topics/benefits/Documents/2011_Emp_Benefits_Report.pdf
[109] **Sleep Foundation:**
https://sleepfoundation.org/sites/default/files/sleepinamericapoll/SIAP_2011_Summary_of_Findings.pdf

[110] **Science Direct:**

http://www.sciencedirect.com/science/article/pii/S0889159117300120

[111] **TIME:**

http://time.com/4672988/the-sleep-cure-fountain-of-youth/

[112] **Labor and Socio-Economic Research Center:**

Effects of Networking on Career Success: A Longitudinal Study. Hans-Georg Wolff University of Erlangen-Nuremberg, Klaus Moser University of Erlangen-Nuremberg. December 2008, LASER Discussion Papers - Paper No. 24, edited by A. Abele-Brehm, R.T. Riphahn, K. Moser and C. Schnabel

[113] **Harvard Business Review:**

https://hbr.org/2011/12/networking-for-survival

[114] **The Chinese Economic Association:**

http://www.ceauk.org.uk/2010-conference-papers/full-papers/Susanne-Ruehle.pdf

[115] **ESB Business School:**

http://www.esb-business school.de/fileadmin/user_upload/Fakultaet_ESB/Forschung/Publikationen/Diskussionsbeitraege_zu_Marketing_Management/Reutlinger_Diskussionsbeitrag_2009_-_6.pdf

[116] **Open Research Online:**

http://oro.open.ac.uk/8711/

[117] **Finances Online:**

https://reviews.financesonline.com/most-popular-social-media-sites-review/

[118] **Forbes:**

https://www.forbes.com/sites/markfidelman/#6b7e97527379

[119] **Wiley:**

http://onlinelibrary.wiley.com/doi/10.1002/smj.507/full

[120] **Harvard Business Review:**

https://hbr.org/2017/07/a-study-shows-how-to-find-new-ideas-inside-and-outside-the-company?utm_source=twitter&utm_medium=social&utm_campaign=hbr

[121] **Sage Journals:**

http://journals.sagepub.com/doi/abs/10.1177/1088868316656701

[122] **Danish Chamber of Commerce:**

Living and working in Denmark An Expat Perspective. Published by Danish Chamber of Commerce and Oxford Research, 2010.

[123] **Nordic Labour Journal:**

http://www.nordiclabourjournal.org/i-fokus/in-focus-2016/trust/article.2016-09-13.8357467929

[124]**The Economist:**

https://www.economist.com/news/special-report/21570835-nordic-countries-are-probably-best-governed-world-secret-their

[125] **Wharton School University of Pennsylvania:**

http://knowledge.wharton.upenn.edu/article/promises-lies-and-apologies-is-it-possible-to-restore-trust-2/

[126] **University of Cambridge Judge Business School:**

http://insight.jbs.cam.ac.uk/2017/ccing-the-boss-can-backfire/

[127] **National Center for Biomedical Information:**

Todorov, A., Funk, F., Olivola, C. Y. (2015). Response to Bonnefon et al,: Limited 'kernels of truth' in facial inferences. Trends in Cognitive Sciences. 19(8), 422-423.

[128] **Eureka Alert:**

https://www.eurekalert.org/pub_releases/2017-05/apa-caw052417.php

[129] **Emerald Insight:**

http://www.emeraldinsight.com/doi/abs/10.1108/01437730710718218

[130] **Edelman:**

http://www.edelman.com/global-results/

[131] **Kronos:**

https://www.kronos.com/SportsWorkBalance/

[132] **Pew Research Centre**:

http://www.pewinternet.org/2014/12/30/email-and-the-internet-are-the-dominant-technological-tools-in-american-workplaces/

[133] **Health Promotion International:**

https://academic.oup.com/heapro/article/28/2/166/661129/Job-autonomy-its-predispositions-and-its-relation

[134] **National Center for Biomedical Information:**

https://www.ncbi.nlm.nih.gov/pubmed/9242799

[135] **Sage Journals:**

http://journals.sagepub.com/doi/pdf/10.1177/0146167216634064

[136] **Glassdoor:**

https://www.glassdoor.com/research/more-money-change-value-at-work/

[137] **Informs:**

http://pubsonline.informs.org/doi/abs/10.1287/mnsc.43.9.1275

[138] **University of Colorado Colorado Springs:**

http://web.uri.edu/iaics/files/S.-P.-Morreale-Shockley-Zalabak.pdf

[139] **Applied Mathematics in Engineering, Management and Technology:**

http://amiemt-journal.com/test/vol3-3/50.pdf

[140] **Organisation for Economic Co-Operation and Development:**

http://www.oecd.org/innovation/research/1825662.pdf

[141] **Research Gate:**

https://www.researchgate.net/publication/211383204_A_Closer_Look_at_Trust_Between_Managers_and_Subordinates_Understanding_the_Effects_of_Both_Trusting_and_Being_Trusted_on_Subordinate_Outcomes

[142] **Environmental Protection Agency:**

https://www.epa.gov/indoor-air-quality-iaq/inside-story-guide-indoor-air-quality

[143] **Environmental Protection Agency:**

https://www.epa.gov/indoor-air-quality-iaq/volatile-organic-compounds-impact-indoor-air-quality

[144] **Sustainable Brands:**

http://www.sustainablebrands.com/news_and_views/new_metrics/sustainable_brands/report_finds_links_between_improved_physical_mental_he

[145] **National Center for Biomedical Information:**

https://www.ncbi.nlm.nih.gov/pmc/articles/PMC5366899/

[146] **New Buildings Institute:**

http://newbuildings.org/sites/default/files/A-9_Windows_Offices_2.6.10.pdf

[147] **D/Science:**
http://www.d-science.nl/wp-content/uploads/sites/2/2015/10/OR10_Daylighting-Bias-and-Biophilia.pdf

[148] **American Psychological Association:**
https://www.psychologie.hu-berlin.de/de/prof/perdev/pdf/2008/Denissen_Weather_Mood_2008.pdf

[149] **National Center for Biomedical Information:**
https://www.ncbi.nlm.nih.gov/pmc/articles/PMC2872309/

[150] **Harvard Business Review:**
https://hbr.org/2017/03/research-stale-office-air-is-making-you-less-productive

[151] **UK Green Building Council:**
http://www.ukgbc.org/sites/default/files/Health%2520Wellbeing%2520and%2520Productivity%2520in%2520Offices%2520%2520The%2520next%2520chapter%2520for%2520green%2520building%2520Full%2520Report_0.pdf

[152] **British Journal of Psychology:**
http://onlinelibrary.wiley.com/doi/10.1111/j.2044-8295.1984.tb02785.x/abstract

[153] **MIND:**
https://www.mind.org.uk/media/336359/Feel-better-outside-feel-better-inside-report.pdf

[154] **Outside Online:**
https://www.outsideonline.com/1870381/take-two-hours-pine-forest-and-call-me-morning

[155] **Sage Journals:**
http://journals.sagepub.com/doi/pdf/10.1177/039463200902200410

[156] **Science Direct:**
http://www.sciencedirect.com/science/article/pii/S0033350606001466

[157] **Human Spaces:**
http://humanspaces.com/report/unique-research-into-biophilic-design-2/

[158] **Science Direct:**
http://www.sciencedirect.com/science/article/pii/S1353829212001220

[159] **The Guardian:**
https://www.theguardian.com/sustainable-business/impact-sea-lakes-rivers-peoples-health

[160] **Employee Volunteering:**
http://employeevolunteering.co.uk/blog/volunteering-strengthens-employee-retention/#_ftn3

[161] **Deloitte:**
https://www2.deloitte.com/global/en/pages/about-deloitte/articles/millennialsurvey.html

[162] **Office for National Statistics:**
https://www.ons.gov.uk/peoplepopulationandcommunity/wellbeing/articles/young peopleswellbeingandpersonalfinance/2017/pdf

[163] **University of Cambridge:**
https://www.educ.cam.ac.uk/research/projects/restorativeapproaches/seminartwo/LEPHALALA%20%20UBUNTU-RA%20-%20PAST%20PRESENT.pdf

[164] **International Journal of Learning & Development:**
Effect of Teamwork on Employee Performance. Sheikh Raheel Manzoor, HafizUllah, Hussain, Kohat KPK, Zulqarnain Muhammad Ahmad. Published: November 24, 2011 Doi:10.5296/ijld.v1i1.1110 URL: http://dx.doi.org/10.5296/ijld.v1i1.1110. International Journal of Learning & Development. ISSN 2164-4063

[165] **Manufacturing and Service Operations Management:**
http://pubsonline.informs.org/doi/abs/10.1287/msom.1080.0233

[166] **The Disney Institute:**
https://disneyinstitute.com/blog/2014/01/the-secret-to-delighting-customers-put-employees-first/

[167] **INC:**
https://www.inc.com/michael-schneider/google-did-an-internal-study-that-will-forever-change-how-they-hire-and-promote-.html?cid=search

[168] **Consortium for Research on Emotional Intelligence in Organizations:**
http://www.eiconsortium.org/reprints/ei_theory_performance.html

[169] **Harvard University:**

Volume: 44 issue: 2, page(s): 350-383, Issue published: June 1, 1999, DOI: https://doi.org/10.2307/2666999, Amy Edmondson, Harvard University

[170] **The Guardian:**

https://www.theguardian.com/us-news/2016/sep/17/american-dream-divided-nation-equal-opportunity-trump-clinton-campaign

[171] **Metro:**

https://metro-co-uk.cdn.ampproject.org/c/metro.co.uk/2017/09/27/firm-hires-a-director-of-happiness-to-retain-the-specialness-of-millennial-employees-6960594/amp/

[172] **University of Warwick:**

Happiness and Productivity. Andrew J. Oswald*, Eugenio Proto, and Daniel Sgroi, University of Warwick, UK, and IZA Bonn, Germany. University of Warwick, UK. JOLE 3rd Version: 10 February 2014

[173] **The Guardian:**

https://www.theguardian.com/science/2010/jul/11/happy-workers-are-more-productive

[174] **Forbes:**

https://www.forbes.com/sites/karstenstrauss/2013/09/08/7-ways-to-keep-your-employees-happy-and-working-really-hard/

[175] **Gallup:**

gallup.com/services/178514/state-American-workplace.aspx & state of the global workforce report

[176] **The Harvard Study of Adult Development Study:**

http://www.adultdevelopmentstudy.org/

[177] **Oprah Online:**

http://www.oprah.com/sp/new-midlife-crisis.html#ixzz4v1VgYYRv

[178] **American Association of Retired Persons:**

http://www.aarp.org/money/credit-loans-debt/info-2015/gen-x-interesting-finance-facts.html

[179] **Princeton University:**
http://wws.princeton.edu/news-and-events/news/item/two-wws-professors-release-new-study-income%E2%80%99s-influence-happiness

[180] **Social Media Week:**
https://socialmediaweek.org/blog/2015/01/83000-new-75000-happiness-benchmark-annual-income/

[181] **Dan Price:**
https://www.linkedin.com/pulse/70k-minimum-wage-has-been-profound-success-failure-two-dan-price/

[182] **Proceedings of the National Academy of Sciences of the United States of America:** http://www.pnas.org/content/114/32/8523

[183] **The Independent:**
http://www.independent.co.uk/news/science/money-buy-happiness-cleaner-cook-gardener-time-stress-a7857731.html

[184] **International Journal of Business and Management:**
http://www.ccsenet.org/journal/index.php/ijbm/article/viewFile/24940/16664

[185] **Sainsbury's:**
https://www.about.sainsburys.co.uk/~/media/Files/S/Sainsburys/living-well-index/sainsburys-living-well-index.PDF

[186] **The Guardian:**
https://www.theguardian.com/money/2010/feb/03/money-worries-britons-stress

[187] **Mintel:**
http://www.mintel.com/press-centre/financial-services/young-free-but-no-spending-spree-half-of-young-brits-worry-about-money-most-of-the-time

[188] **American Psychological Association:**
http://www.apa.org/news/press/releases/stress/index.aspx

[189] **Barclays:**
https://wealth.barclays.com/global-stock-and-rewards/en_gb/home/research-centre/financial-wellbeing.html

[190] **National Center for Biotechnology Information:**
https://www.ncbi.nlm.nih.gov/pmc/articles/PMC2921311/

[191] **The Reward and Employee Benefits Association:**
http://reba.global/reports/report-global-employee-benefits-watch-2016-17-2
[192] **HR Grapevine:**
https://www.hrgrapevine.com/content/article/1970-01-01-uk-smes-spend-up-to-950-million-annually-on-employee-benefits
[193] **MetLife:**
https://benefittrends.metlife.com/
[194] **Towers Watson:**
https://www.towerswatson.com/en/insights/newsletters/americas/insider/2014/attracting-and-keeping-employees-strategic-value-of-employee-benefits
[195] **Employee Benefits:**
https://www.employeebenefits.co.uk/issues/benefits-research-2017/employee-benefitsstaffcare-benefits-research-2017/
[196] **CNBC:**
https://www.cnbc.com/2017/04/11/the-number-of-americans-without-health-insurance-rose-in-first-quarter-2017.html
[197] **Employee Benefit Research Institute:**
https://www.ebri.org/publications/notes/index.cfm?fa=notesDisp&content_id=3443
[198] **Employee Benefit Research Institute:**
https://www.ebri.org/publications/notes/index.cfm?fa=notesDisp&content_id=3299
[199] **Aflac:**
https://www.aflac.com/docs/awr/pdf/2017-articles/z170697-millennials_final.pdf
[200] **Cancer Research UK:**
http://www.cancerresearchuk.org/health-professional/cancer-statistics/incidence/age
[201] **ResearchMoz:**
http://www.digitaljournal.com/pr/3530930#.We99zsNdduo.linkedin
[202] **Professional Pensions:**
https://www.professionalpensions.com/professional-pensions/feature/3006198/how-employee-benefits-for-smes-are-changing

[203] **MetLife:**

https://benefittrends.metlife.com/

[204] **DEPUTY:**

https://www.deputy.com/blog/why-are-so-many-australians-late-to-work

[205] **News.AU:**

http://www.news.com.au/finance/work/at-work/australias-hardest-working-state-revealed/news-story/353727e037c28edcc8de89ffc30f0a97

[206] **The Herald Sun:**

http://www.heraldsun.com.au/news/victoria/schools-wake-up-to-sleepy-students-and-consider-later-teaching-hours/news-story/ca9fb3b52920d4afd43875007250d6cd

[207] **The National Center for Biotechnology Information Advances Science and Health:**

Boergers J[1], Gable CJ, Owens JA. J Dev Behav Pediatr. 2014 Jan;35(1):11-7. doi: 10.1097/DBP.0000000000000018. The National Center for Biotechnology Information advances science and health

[208] **Sleep:**

Basner M, Spaeth Am, Dinges DF. Sociodemographic Characteristics and Waking Activities and their Role in the Timing and Duration of Sleep. Sleep. Published online December 10, 2014

[209] **National Center for Chronic Disease Prevention and Health Promotion:**

Prevalence of Healthy Sleep Duration among Adults — United States, 2014. National Center for Chronic Disease Prevention and Health Promotion, CDCYong Liu, MD[1]; Anne G. Wheaton, PhD[1]; Daniel P. Chapman, PhD[1]; Timothy J. Cunningham, ScD[1]; Hua Lu, MS[1]; Janet B. Croft, PhD[1]

[210] **The Guardian:**

https://www.theguardian.com/lifeandstyle/2012/apr/01/chronic-sleep-deprivation-uk-staff

[211] **RAND:**

Hafner, Marco, Martin Stepanek, Jirka Taylor, Wendy M. Troxel and Christian Van Stolk. Why sleep matters — the economic costs of insufficient sleep: A cross-country comparative analysis. Santa Monica, CA: RAND Corporation, 2016.

[212] **Academy of Management Review:**

http://amr.aom.org/content/early/2017/04/13/amr.2015.0185.abstract

[213] **The Huffington Post:**

http://www.huffingtonpost.co.uk/entry/night-owls-should-be-allowed-to-work-later-study-suggests_uk_5922b6a9e4b034684b0d8e26?ir=UK+Tech&

[214] **Thrive Global:**

https://www.thriveglobal.com/stories/10718-a-worthy-walk

[215] **Benefit News:**

https://www.benefitnews.com/news/avoidable-turnover-costing-employers-big?brief=00000152-14a7-d1cc-a5fa-7cffccf00000

[216] **Business Wire:**

http://www.businesswire.com/news/home/20160407005736/en/Quality-Work-Life-Worth-7600-Pay-Cut

[217] **The Daily Mail:**

http://www.dailymail.co.uk/sciencetech/article-4945486/People-work-home-productive.html

[218] **Jacob Morgan – The Future If:**

https://www.linkedin.com/pulse/flexible-work-future-ofwork-jacob-morgan/

[219] **HR Review:**

http://www.hrreview.co.uk/hr-news/tuc-says-flexible-working-requests-can-end-worse-outcomes/105684

[220] **BT:**

https://www2.bt.com/static/i/media/pdf/flex_working_wp_07.pdf

[221] **Pew Research Centre:**

Technology Device Ownership: 2015. Pew Research Centre, October 2015

[222] **Daily Mail:**

http://www.dailymail.co.uk/news/article-1304266/We-spend-7-hours-day-using-technology-computers-TV-lives.html#ixzz4ZPvMMWxv

[223] **Behaviour & Information Technology:** Workplace user frustration with computers: an exploratory investigation of the causes and severity. Jonathan Lazar, Adam Jones and Ben Shneiderman. Dept. of Computer and Information Sciences, Centre for Applied Information Technology and Universal Usability Laboratory, Towson University, Maryland, US. Dept. of Computer Science, Human-Computer Interaction Laboratory, Institute for Advanced Computer Studies and Institute for Systems Research, University of Maryland, US. Behaviour & Information Technology, Vol. 25, No. 3, May–June 2006, 239 – 251

[224] **New York Times:**
http://www.nytimes.com/2012/03/01/technology/impatient-web-users-flee-slow-loading-sites.html

[225] **The Mirror Online:**
http://www.mirror.co.uk/tech/brits-patience-tech-lasts-just-8351696

[226] **University of Maryland:**
User Frustration with Technology in the Workplace (2004). Lazar, Jonathan - Jones, Adam - Bessiere, Katie - Ceaparu, Irina - Shneiderman, Ben. University of Maryland, College Park

[227] **Netspoke:**
https://www.netskope.com/wp-content/uploads/2014/07/NS-Cloud-Report-Jul14-RS-00.pdf

[228] **PwC:**
https://www.pwc.in/assets/pdfs/industries/technology/thefutureofitoutsourcingandcloudcomputing.pdf

[229] **Cornerstone OnDemand:**
https://www.cornerstoneondemand.com/resources/research/state-of-workplace-productivity-2013

[230] **Salesforce:**
https://www.salesforce.com/form/pdf/state-of-the-connected-customer.jsp?d=7010M000000NkvP&nc=7010M000000NlIY

[231] **Pew Research Centre:**
http://www.pewinternet.org/2014/12/30/email-and-the-internet-are-the-dominant-technological-tools-in-american-workplaces/

[232] **TriNet:**
https://www.trinet.com/documents/eguides/trinet_eguide_improve_business_performance_with_hr_technology.pdf
[233] **Deloitte:**
https://dupress.deloitte.com/dup-us-en/focus/human-capital-trends.html
[234] **The Green Building Information Gateway**
http://insight.gbig.org/smart-building-tech-not-just-about-people/
[235] **CIO Dive:**
http://www.ciodive.com/news/the-future-workplace-smart-offices-electronic-communication-and-high-te/422775/
[236] **Business Insider:**
http://www.businessinsider.com/americans-are-spending-more-on-their-gadgets-than-are-on-heating-their-homes-2012-1?IR=T
[237] **The Disney Institute:**
https://disneyinstitute.com/blog/2014/01/the-secret-to-delighting-customers-put-employees-first/
[238] **National Center for Biotechnology Information:**
https://www.ncbi.nlm.nih.gov/pubmed/16484496
[239] **Pearson Lab:**
http://www.pearsonlab.org/images/human_intuition.pdf
[240] **SSRN:**
https://papers.ssrn.com/sol3/papers.cfm?abstract_id=394920
[241] **National Center for Biotechnology Information:**
https://www.ncbi.nlm.nih.gov/pubmed/9036851
[242] **National Center for Biotechnology Information:**
https://www.ncbi.nlm.nih.gov/pubmed/21280961
[243] **ERIC:**
https://eric.ed.gov/?id=EJ980465
[244] **Science Direct:**
http://www.sciencedirect.com/science/article/pii/S0148296314000885

[245] **Research Gate:**
https://www.researchgate.net/profile/Lisa_Burke-Smalley/publication/279400692_Taking_the_mystery_out_of_intuitive_decision_making/links/570f7d1a08ae170055bc571f/Taking-the-mystery-out-of-intuitive-decision-making.pdf

[246] **JAN:**
http://onlinelibrary.wiley.com/doi/10.1046/j.1365-2648.1997.1997026194.x/full

[247] **Fast Company:**
https://www.fastcompany.com/3030659/less-is-more-why-youre-saying-too-much-and-getting-ignored

[248] **Pew Research Centre:**
http://www.pewinternet.org/2014/12/30/email-and-the-internet-are-the-dominant-technological-tools-in-american-workplaces/

[249] **Esquire:**
http://www.esquire.com/entertainment/movies/a55985/christopher-nolan-interview/

[250] **Journal of Occupational Health Psychology:**
Please Respond ASAP: Workplace Telepressure and Employee Recovery Larissa K. Barber and Alecia M. Santuzzi Online First Publication, November 3, 2014.

[251] **Ofcom:**
https://www.ofcom.org.uk/about-ofcom/latest/media/media-releases/2011/a-nation-addicted-to-smartphones

[252] **Ofcom:**
https://www.ofcom.org.uk/about-ofcom/latest/media/media-releases/2011/a-nation-addicted-to-smartphones

[253] **School Effectiveness and Inequality Initiative:**
https://news.utexas.edu/2017/06/26/the-mere-presence-of-your-smartphone-reduces-brain-power

[254] **Donald Bren School of Information and Computer Sciences:**
https://www.ics.uci.edu/~gmark/chi08-mark.pdf

[255] **The Daily Mail:**

http://www.dailymail.co.uk/health/article-3310195/Rise-smartphone-injuries-43-people-walked-glued-screen-60-dropped-phone-face-reading.html

[256] **The Telegraph:**

http://www.macon.com/news/local/community/houston-peach/article174940366.html

[257] **The Telegraph:**

http://www.telegraph.co.uk/technology/2016/02/22/half-the-planet-will-need-glasses-by-2050-because-of-screens/

[258] **The Mirror:**

http://www.mirror.co.uk/news/uk-news/millions-brits-switch-social-media-10832935

[259] **BBC:**

http://www.bbc.co.uk/news/health-39955295

[260] **Mary Ann Libert Inc.:**

http://online.liebertpub.com/doi/full/10.1089/cyber.2016.0530

[261] **The Independent:**

http://www.independent.co.uk/news/education/education-news/child-smart-phones-cocaine-addiction-expert-mandy-saligari-harley-street-charter-clinic-technology-a7777941.html

[262] **ZDNet:**

http://www.zdnet.com/article/phone-sex-using-our-smartphones-from-the-shower-to-the-sack/

[263] **New York University:**

http://www.nyu.edu/classes/keefer/waoe/miakotkol.pdf

[264] **University of California:**

https://www.ics.uci.edu/~gmark/chi08-mark.pdf

[265] **Mashable:**

http://mashable.com/2012/08/01/email-workers-time/#Qv5iMwgbnEqV

[266] **The Radicati Group, Inc.:**

http://www.radicati.com/wp/wp-content/uploads/2011/05/Email-Statistics-Report-2011-2015-Executive-Summary.pdf

[267] **School Effectiveness and Inequality Initiative:**
https://seii.mit.edu/wp-content/uploads/2016/05/SEII-Discussion-Paper-2016.02-Payne-Carter-Greenberg-and-Walker-2.pdf

[268] **International Labour Organisations**:
Travail Legal Database: Working Time in the European Region". Travail: Conditions of Work and Employment Programme. International Labour Organisations, September 2014.

[269] **CIPD:**
http://www2.cipd.co.uk/pm/peoplemanagement/b/weblog/archive/2013/08/19/third-of-workers-not-taking-full-holiday-entitlement.aspx

[270] **Project Timeoff:**
http://www.projecttimeoff.com/research/work-martyrs-cautionary-tale

[271] **Small Business:**
http://smallbusiness.co.uk/uk-workers-putting-13-extra-days-work-year-2540914/

[272] **Applied Research in Quality of Life:**
Nawijn J, Marchand MA, Veenhoven R, Vingerhoets AJ. Vacationers Happier, but Most not Happier After a Holiday. Applied Research in Quality of Life. 2010;5(1):35-47. doi:10.1007/s11482-009-9091-9.)

[273] **Grethen Rubin:**
http://gretchenrubin.com/happiness_project/2007/08/a-key-to-happ-2

[274] **American Journal of Epidemiology:**
Myocardial Infarction and Coronary Death among Women: Psychosocial Predictors from a 20-Year Follow-up of Women in the Framingham Study, Elaine D. Eaker, Joan Pinsky, William P. Castelli, Am J Epidemiol (1992) 135 (8): 854-864, 15 April 1992.).

[275] **Leisure Sciences:**
Moderating Effects of Vacation on Reactions to Work and Domestic Stress. Gerhard Strauss-Blasche, Cem Ekmekcioglu, and Wolfgang Marktl, Leisure Sciences Vol. 24 , Iss. 2,2002.

[276] **The Washington Post:**
http://apps.washingtonpost.com/g/documents/local/vacation-collective-restoration-and-mental-health-in-a-population/1167/

[277] **New York Daily News:**

http://www.nydailynews.com/news/national/americans-travel-survey-article-1.2431648

[278] **LA Times:**

http://articles.latimes.com/2013/dec/17/news/la-trb-travel-best-medicine-study-20131217

[279] **American Psychological Association:**

http://www.apa.org/pubs/journals/releases/rev-1091116.pdf

[280] **Sage Journals:**

http://journals.sagepub.com/doi/abs/10.1177/0956797614546556

[281] **American Psychological Association:**

http://psycnet.apa.org/record/1996-04477-003

[282] **HR Grapevine:**

https://www.hrgrapevine.com/content/article/news-2017-10-31-lidl-worker-canned-for-working-too-hard?utm_source=linkedin&utm_medium=social&utm_content=Oktopost-linkedin-profile&utm_campaign=Oktopost-HR+LinkedIn+Page

[283] **Organisation for Economic Cooperation and Development:**

http://www.oecd-ilibrary.org/industry-and-services/oecd-compendium-of-productivity-indicators_22252126

[284] **Project Timeoff:**

https://www.projecttimeoff.com/sites/default/files/StateofAmericanVacation2017.pdf

[285] **Project Timeoff:**

https://www.projecttimeoff.com/sites/default/files/StateofAmericanVacation2017.pdf

[286] **Sage Journals:**

Inspired by Distraction: Mind Wandering Facilitates Creative Incubation. Benjamin Baird, Jonathan Smallwood, Michael D. Mrazek, Julia W. Y. Kam, Michael S.Franklin, Jonathan W. Schooler. First Published August 31, 2012

[287] **The New York Times:**
https://www.nytimes.com/2017/10/05/world/asia/japan-death-overwork.html?_r=0
[288] **The Ministry of Health, Labor, and Welfare:**
The Ministry of Health, Labor, and Welfare, 2016
[289] **AIA The Real Life Company:**
http://www.aia.com/en/healthy-living/the-healthiest-workplace.html
[290] **The Independent:**
http://www.independent.co.uk/news/world/asia/japan-three-day-weekend-company-yahoo-japan-corp-overtime-hours-overwork-dentsu-mintsubishi-a7526101.html
[291] **Gallup:**
'The "40-Hour" Workweek Is Actually Longer – by seven hours', L. Saad, Gallup, August 2014
[292] **Recode:**
https://www.recode.net/2017/5/25/15690106/gig-on-demand-economy-workers-doubling-uber
[293] **Harvard Business Review:**
'Making Time Off Predictable – and Required', L. A. Perlow, J. L. Porter, Harvard Business Review, October 2009).
[294] **The Lancet:**
'Long working hours and risk of coronary heart disease and stroke: a systematic review and meta-analysis of published and unpublished data for 603 838 individuals'. Prof Mika Kivimäki, PhD, et al. The Lancet, Vol. 386, No. 10005, October 2015
[295] **Melbourne Institute:**
http://melbourneinstitute.unimelb.edu.au/
[296] **NORC at the University of Chicago:**
http://gss.norc.org/
[297] **University of California School of Sociology:**
http://faculty.sites.uci.edu/pressman/publications/
[298] **Harvard Business Review:**
https://hbr.org/2013/03/goodbye-to-flexible-work

[299] **CultureRX:**
https://d3aencwbm6zmht.cloudfront.net/asset/206719/Gap_Inc_Case_Study.pdf
[300] **Business Insider:**
http://www.businessinsider.com/rowe-culture-could-close-gender-gap-2013-7?IR=T
[301] **HR Grapevine:**
https://www.hrgrapevine.com/content/article/insight-2017-09-19-could-annualised-hours-lift-productivity?utm_source=twitter&utm_medium=social&utm_content=Oktopost-twitter-profile&utm_campaign=Oktopost-HR+Twitter#.WcOadzl4TV0.twitter
[302] **American Psychological Association:**
http://psycnet.apa.org/index.cfm?fa=buy.optionToBuy&id=2001-07409-008
[303] **UK Business Insider:**
http://uk.businessinsider.com/tricks-stores-use-to-make-you-spend-more-money-2015-10
[304] **Cognitive Emotion:**
Dubé, L. & Le Bel, J. The content and structure of laypeople's concept of pleasure. Cognition Emotion 17, 263–295 (2003).
[305] **Public Library of Science:**
http://journals.plos.org/plosone/article?id=10.1371/journal.pone.0094446
[306] **Science Direct:**
https://www.sciencedirect.com/science/article/pii/0003687072901019?np=y
[307] **Neuroscience Letters:**
https://www.uwosh.edu/psychology/faculty-and-staff/frances-rauscher-ph.d/Rauscher_ShawKy_1995.pdf
[308] **Sage Journals:**
http://journals.sagepub.com/doi/abs/10.1177/1029864911398065
[309] **Belief, Perception and Cognition Lab:**
http://www.jolij.com/?p=362
[310] **National Centre for Biotechnology Information:**
Cockerton, T., Moore, S., & Norman, D. (1997). Cognitive test performance and background music. PERCEPTUAL AND MOTOR SKILLS, 85, 1435-1438.).

[311] **Sage Journals:**
http://journals.sagepub.com/doi/abs/10.1177/0305735616659552
[312] **Sage Journals:**
http://journals.sagepub.com/doi/abs/10.1177/0305735614536754
[313] **National Centre for Biotechnology Information:**
https://www.ncbi.nlm.nih.gov/pubmed/19388893
[314] **Science Direct:**
http://www.sciencedirect.com/science/article/pii/S1524904210001396
[315] **National Centre for Biotechnology Information:**
https://www.ncbi.nlm.nih.gov/pubmed/10052073
[316] **National Centre for Biotechnology Information:**
https://www.ncbi.nlm.nih.gov/m/pubmed/22176481/
[317] **National Centre for Biotechnology Information:**
https://www.ncbi.nlm.nih.gov/pubmed/15135879
[318] **National Centre for Biotechnology Information:**
https://www.ncbi.nlm.nih.gov/pubmed/17454575
[319] **CIPD:**
http://www2.cipd.co.uk/pm/peoplemanagement/b/weblog/archive/2017/09/07/majority-of-hr-professionals-believe-music-is-motivational-at-work.aspx
[320] **Scientific American:**
https://www.scientificamerican.com/article/why-does-music-make-us-fe/
[321] **Emerald Insight:**
http://www.emeraldinsight.com/toc/f/21/1%2F2
[322] **The Conference Board:**
https://www.conference-board.org/publications/publicationdetail.cfm?publicationid=2785¢erId=4
[323] **Gensler:**
https://www.gensler.com/uploads/documents/Focus_in_the_Workplace_10_01_2012.pdf
[324] **Science Direct:**
http://www.sciencedirect.com/science/article/pii/S2212567115005249

[325] **HR Summits:**

https://hrsummits.co.uk/half-of-britisot-good-enough/?

[326] **Journal of Experimental Psychology:**

https://adobe99u.files.wordpress.com/2013/07/2010+jep+space+experiments.pdf

[327] **Journal of Experimental Psychology:**

https://adobe99u.files.wordpress.com/2013/07/2010+jep+space+experiments.pdf

[328] **Personality and Social Psychology Bulletin:**

https://adobe99u.files.wordpress.com/2013/07/2012_lichtenfeldetal_pspb.pdf

[329] **National Centre for Biotechnology Information:**

https://www.ncbi.nlm.nih.gov/pmc/articles/PMC3743993/

[330] **National Centre for Biotechnology Information:**

https://www.ncbi.nlm.nih.gov/pmc/articles/PMC3757288/

[331] **National Centre for Biotechnology Information:**

https://www.ncbi.nlm.nih.gov/pmc/articles/PMC3757288/

[332] **Gensler:**

https://www.gensler.com/uploads/documents/2013_US_Workplace_Survey_07_15_2013.pdf

[333] **National Public Radio (TED):**

http://www.npr.org/templates/transcript/transcript.php?storyId=283464243

[334] **Science Direct:**

http://www.sciencedirect.com/science/article/pii/S0272494415300293

[335] **Sage Journals:**

http://journals.sagepub.com/doi/abs/10.1177/0013916502034003001

[336] **American Psychological Association:**

https://adobe99u.files.wordpress.com/2013/07/2010+jep+space+experiments.pdf

[337] **Academy of Management Journal:**

http://www.jstor.org/stable/255498?seq=1#page_scan_tab_contents

[338] **Journal of Applied Psychology:**

http://psycnet.apa.org/journals/apl/85/5/779/

[339] **National Centre for Biotechnology Information:**

https://www.ncbi.nlm.nih.gov/pubmed/21528171

[340] **Harvard Business Review:**
https://hbr.org/2017/02/want-to-be-more-productive-sit-next-to-someone-who-is
[341] **Harvard Business Review:**
https://hbr.org/2017/02/want-to-be-more-productive-sit-next-to-someone-who-is
[342] **Up Desk:**
https://www.myupdesk.com/blog/sitting-is-the-new-smoking-and-it-may-lead-to-lawsuits
[343] **The Guardian:**
https://www.theguardian.com/money/2014/oct/06/workers-take-time-off-care-children-elderly-relatives
[344] **CIPD:**
http://www2.cipd.co.uk/pm/peoplemanagement/b/weblog/archive/2016/08/26/employees-using-sick-leave-to-care-for-elderly-relatives.aspx
[345] **CIPD:**
https://www.cipd.co.uk/knowledge/culture/well-being/enabling-carers
[346] **Caregiver:**
https://www.caregiver.org/caregiver-statistics-work-and-caregiving
[347] **AARP:**
https://assets.aarp.org/rgcenter/ppi/ltc/i51-caregiving.pdf
[348] **Georgetown University Law Center:**
http://scholarship.law.georgetown.edu/cgi/viewcontent.cgi?article=1011&context=legal
[349] **Working Families:**
https://www.workingfamilies.org.uk/wp-content/uploads/2014/09/Flexible-Working-Performance-2008.pdf
[350] **National Centre for Biotechnology Information:**
https://www.ncbi.nlm.nih.gov/pmc/articles/PMC3905922/
[351] **Science Daily:**
https://www.sciencedaily.com/releases/2008/02/080215135707.htm
[352] **CNN:**
http://edition.cnn.com/2015/04/09/health/creativity-socializing-delay-dementia/index.html

[353] **AARP:**

http://www.aarp.org/health/brain-health/info-11-2008/friends-are-good-for-your-brain.html

[354] **Highland Spring Group:**

http://www.highlandspringgroup.com/press-and-media/group-news/article/34-minutes-the-amount-of-time-the-average-family-gets-to-spend-together-each-day/

[355] **The National Centre on Addiction and Substance Abuse**:

https://www.centeronaddiction.org/newsroom/press-releases/2010-family-dinners-report-finds

[356] **Penn State College of Health and Human Development:**

http://hhd.psu.edu/hdfs/frp/research

[357] **Penn State College of Health and Human Development:**

http http://hhd.psu.edu/hdfs/frp/research

[358] **Stress and Health Journal:**

http://onlinelibrary.wiley.com/doi/10.1002/smi.1049/full

[359] https://www2.bt.com/static/i/media/pdf/flex_working_wp_07.pdf

[360] **UK Government:**

https://www.gov.uk/government/statistics/announcements/english-housing-survey-2016-to-2017-headline-report

[361] **Live Science:**

https://www.livescience.com/9824-5-happier.html

[362] **Review of General Psychology:**

http://sonjalyubomirsky.com/wp-content/themes/sonjalyubomirsky/papers/LSS2005.pdf

[363] **INC:**

https://www-inc-com.cdn.ampproject.org/c/s/www.inc.com/amp/167276.html

[364] **LinkedIn:**

https://www.linkedin.com/pulse/most-liked-articles-all-times-linkedin-100000-likes-vishnepolsky/?trackingId=n0j83mjzVNcx5Qfl5762aw%3D%3D&lipi=urn%3Ali%3Apage%3Ad_flagship3_feed%3ByhYWH3RBRvGzW3MhvMS7eg%3D%3D&licu=urn%3Ali%3Acontrol%3Ad_flagship3_feed-object

[365] **Morning Consult Intelligence:**
https://morningconsultintelligence.com/featured/2017/6/12/admired-employer
[366] **IBM Smarter Workforce Institute & Work Human Research Institute:**
The Employee Experience Index – A new measure of human workplace and its impact', IBM Smarter Workforce Institute & Work Human Research Institute, 2017
[367] **World Health Organisation:**
http://www.who.int/mental_health/evidence/en/promoting_mhh.pdf
[368] **Human Experience:**
http://humanexperience.jll/?lipi=urn%3Ali%3Apage%3Ad_flagship3_pulse_read%3BUYxXc5w%2BR%2FiW7jqYB2bHQg%3D%3D
[369] **Clinical Infectious Diseases:**
https://academic.oup.com/cid/article-lookup/doi/10.1093/cid/cir773
[370] **CNBC:**
https://www.cnbc.com/2017/05/09/6-lessons-from-disney-ceo-bob-iger-on-creating-corporate-magic.html
[372] **National Centre for Biotechnology Information:**
Open Hearts Build Lives: Positive Emotions, Induced Through Loving-Kindness Meditation, Build Consequential Personal Resources**'**, Barbara L. Fredrickson. J Pers Soc Psychol. 2008 Nov; 95(5): 1045–1062., doi: 10.1037/a0013262
[373] **American Psychological Association:**
http://www.apa.org/monitor/jun06/learning.aspx
[374] **On Office Magazine:**
https://www.onofficemagazine.com/interiors/item/4671-the-secret-to-workplace-happiness
[375] **National Centre for Biotechnology Information:**
https://www.ncbi.nlm.nih.gov/pmc/articles/PMC1519413/
[376] **Mercola:**
https://articles.mercola.com/sites/articles/archive/2015/12/03/flourishing-emotionally-positivity-ratio.aspx
[377] **The American Institute of Stress:**
https://www.stress.org/americas-1-health-problem/

[378] **Sky News:**
http://news.sky.com/story/work-causes-mental-health-issues-in-60-of-employees-11066428?lipi=urn%3Ali%3Apage%3Ad_flagship3_detail_base%3BhLJKLIJJSmKuNchRiV9qiA%3D%3D

[379] **Sky News:**
http://news.sky.com/story/work-causes-mental-health-issues-in-60-of-employees-11066428?lipi=urn%3Ali%3Apage%3Ad_flagship3_detail_base%3BhLJKLIJJSmKuNchRiV9qiA%3D%3D

[380] **American Psychological Association:**
http://www.apa.org/news/press/releases/stress/2014/stress-report.pdf

[381] **BioMed Central:**
https://bmcpublichealth.biomedcentral.com/articles/10.1186/1471-2458-11-642

[382] **Science Direct:**
http://www.sciencedirect.com/science/article/pii/S1048984311001263

[383] **National Centre for Biotechnology Information:**
https://www.ncbi.nlm.nih.gov/pubmed/21875210

[384] **FullFact:**
https://fullfact.org/economy/whos-working-gig-economy/

[385] **FullFact:**
https://fullfact.org/economy/whos-working-gig-economy/

[385] **Academy of Management:**
http://amj.aom.org/content/56/6/1601.abstract

[385] **Forbes:**
https://www.forbes.com/sites/amymorin/2014/11/23/7-scientifically-proven-benefits-of-gratitude-that-will-motivate-you-to-give-thanks-year-round/#4ac807a0183c

[385] **Oxford Academic:**
https://academic.oup.com/cercor/article/10/3/295/449599/Emotion-Decision-Making-and-the-Orbitofrontal

[385] **Western Journal of Communication:**
http://www.unm.edu/~plutgen/Employees%20Best-Work%20Experiences.pdf

[385] **American Psychological Association:**
http://www.apa.org/monitor/mar06/employees.aspx
[385] **American Psychological Association:**
http://www.apa.org/news/press/releases/2015/03/healthy-workplace.aspx
[386] **Academy of Management:**
http://amj.aom.org/content/56/6/1601.abstract
[387] **Forbes:**
https://www.forbes.com/sites/amymorin/2014/11/23/7-scientifically-proven-benefits-of-gratitude-that-will-motivate-you-to-give-thanks-year-round/#4ac807a0183c
[388] **Oxford Academic:**
https://academic.oup.com/cercor/article/10/3/295/449599/Emotion-Decision-Making-and-the-Orbitofrontal
[389] **Western Journal of Communication:**
http://www.unm.edu/~plutgen/Employees%20Best-Work%20Experiences.pdf
[390] **Science Direct:**
http://www.sciencedirect.com/science/article/pii/S0092656603000588
[391] **Glassdoor:**
https://www.glassdoor.co.uk/employers/blog/the-cost-of-a-disengaged-employee/
[392] **HR Grapevine:**
https://www.hrgrapevine.com/content/article/feature-2017-09-26-why-starbucks-hires-for-attitude-and-not-experience
[393] **Oxford Academic:**
https://academic.oup.com/ojls/article/35/4/665/2472464/To-Blame-or-to-Forgive-Reconciling-Punishment-and
[394] **Scientific American:**
https://www.scientificamerican.com/article/the-happy-couple-2012-10-23/
[395] **Harvard University:**
https://www.health.harvard.edu/newsletter_article/in-praise-of-gratitude
[396] **City AM:**
http://www.cityam.com/274143/these-top-20-uk-companies-best-workplace-culture

[397] **American Psychological Association:**

http://www.apa.org/monitor/mar06/employees.aspx

[398] **American Psychological Association:**

http://www.apa.org/news/press/releases/2015/03/healthy-workplace.aspx

Manufactured by Amazon.ca
Bolton, ON

21043672R00155